HOW TO FALL IN LOVE

Tips on how to choose the right guy

TONY RICH

Table of Contents

INTRODUCTION

Have you ever had issues finding the right guy? Maybe, you find it hard to find a guy at all; or you always go for the wrong type. Then again, perhaps he is the right kind, but then you see him running away from you at full speed as soon as the train's touched down at the next station. You never seem to get past the 'honeymoon' stage in your relationship, and it keeps running into a dead-end relationship. What you found to be a beautiful and glamorous beginning ends up an ugly performance, which ends in tears and humiliation. The curtain falls, and time and time again, you are left with no hope of getting to the next stage - a serious, loving relationship with memories to last a lifetime or even just a few years. However, no one wants to be single forever!

Equally, no one wants to see themselves in a toxic, loveless relationship that is out to destroy everything in its path and carry you away at the end, as the beaten prize. You are the maker of your own destiny. Therefore, if you want to live a happy and fulfilled life, then you must fulfill it with someone who does want the best for you. Who also appreciates you and loves you for being you, even when the 'honeymoon' romance wears out. You cannot get confused and think that this is the end of a relationship because it's just beginning. Although, it is natural for you to get wrapped up in the adrenalin and excitement felt when you first meet and get to know one other. However, it slowly starts to wear out because you get comfortable together, yet at the same time, this comfort is supposed to support you, unlike any other. So, as long as you can learn to adapt to change and not leap off at the first fall, then you should be fine.

Love is a tied web of complex orders, yet there's still order to it, as long as you are aware of the logistics, then you can make your own set of rules and guidelines, which you can use for personal reference. Once you can make sense of these and implement them to your love life, only then will you be able to discover and stay happy in love. Whatever you do, never fall into a pattern of victimization.

Then for those of you living with someone who finds it hard to communicate, you have to be wary not to force information out of them. Men have different ways of communicating their feelings, other than women. A better understanding of the ways that men deal with stress allows for a better appreciation of the love and support that they can provide in a relationship, especially when you give them a chance. Life is full of challenges that you can master when you can learn to work together as a team. Take time to get to know one another and look after each other, but also never let him think he has control over you.

Love is a powerful force when it reaches a perfect harmony, only then can you start imagining, maybe not your honeymoon together with them anymore. Instead, you have your future as a retired couple growing old and holding hands with a book full of tales to tell your grandkids and memories made to last a lifetime.

Chapter 1

FINDING THAT SPECIAL SOMEONE

"He loves, he loves me not... he loves me!"
(Ariel, Little Mermaid, 1989)

Do you remember those days, when you were young and sitting on the grass bank with your girlfriends from school? What was it that you used to talk about? Did you discuss your homework? Or maybe, your hopes and dreams? Or did you talk about boys? Boys, boys, and more boys!

You might have had a science book open on your lap, whilst you were trying to study for your all-important upcoming exams. However, had you been concentrating, or taking anything in? I doubt it! I believe that many of us, although we may regret it now were probably sat there in a daze daydreaming about a guy. He may have been a famous pop star or the new kid in town. Unknown to us, time and time again, they would uncontrollably pop back into our minds and take over our thoughts completely. No matter how many times you kept reading the page, repeatedly, you were never reading it or registering any of the information. You could have been reading another language!

Your head is always elsewhere, scoping out a frame for your romantic fantasies, so they can be left to reenact in your mind until they seem real. Then out of the corner of your eye, you catch sight of a beautiful blooming flower. It is so colorful and bright that it entices you to pick it up out the ground. It reminds you of the beauty to be in love, so you begin to mimic your favorite underwater fairytale tale character, Ariel, after she meets the man of her dreams, Prince Eric. You pick at the petals one by one, plucking them away and discarding them to the floor. All the while, the words ring through your thoughts, "he loves me, he loves me not, he loves me!"

We cannot help feeling a sudden rush of hope and expectation at the revelation when we land on the last petal with 'he loves me!' Yet, does it always come true? Can we obtain love in a 50/50 lucky draw; or measure it on a scale of 1 - 10? Is love really measurable at all? Is it a still entity, or does it shift and move, slowly growing or sometimes falling apart?

The truth is, I think love is more complicated than we ever imagined it to be. Take Hans Christian Anderson's Little Mermaid, who falls in love with a human when she is not supposed to go on land. I think this is emblematic of people who fall in love. We cannot help who we fall in love with, but also we can't help falling for a challenge or sometimes, even the impossible! We want what we cannot have. We will also try all measures to obtain it. The only problem, is how? What if he has a girlfriend? Maybe, it was not us who showed interest at first, but them. However, once you have fallen for their charm and you start to show them some attention back, they are running a mile. The challenge has gone and so has their interest. How can you get back their interest? These are just a few issues I will be addressing in this first chapter, 'Finding that special someone.'

There is no need to worry anymore or be asking yourself the same unanswered questions, as you go turning the pages to this book, I will be letting you into some well sought-after secrets. Once you are aware of these, then love and your relationship goals will start to look less complicated and they will slowly start to fall into place. Like everything in life, there is a set of rules or guidelines you should follow, which will get you further and faster to your goal. It is important to be aware of them and put them into practice without going off track. Although, you may be tempted to act on impulse or passionate emotions. However, you often meet complicated and sticky situations by acting purely on emotive thoughts, rather than logical ones.

However, before the relationship gets wind of developing into something more complicated, then we must cross step one first and win over our dream guy! Now, if you do not have someone really impossible in mind, like Tom Hardy or George Clooney, where you might be thinking a little too far off the spectrum. I'm afraid, unless you want to consider taking up a career in Hollywood or attempt competing with one of the beautiful mannequin models stood by their side; you are have a very small, if not no chance. However, if you have someone relatively realistic in mind, then start by reading this handful of helpful tips I have mapped out in this first chapter to winning over your dream man. As you go reading take careful note, what you must do and what you must not do...

Don't forget love is not about picking the lucky straw, you make your own luck. Instead, you could look at love, like a game of cards, or Texas Holdem Poker. Without needing to go into an in-depth look at the logistics, or rules of the game. Imagine that you've been taught the rules like I am going to teach you with this book about love. Once you know them and start putting them into place, then no matter what luck you're given, or even if the game doesn't go to plan, it's okay. Just make sure you keep your cool and work discretely with your opponent, that way you're sure to win. You just have to learn to play their bluff! Sit back, relax and read. Don't lose hope at winning the man you've been after all this time, as he's only a few steps away; once you put these helpful guidelines in place.

1.1 What is it about them

"Je ne sais quoi" - 'I don't know what' in French
(Anonymous)

So, what is it about them in the first place? How do we define those feelings we have for that special someone that's been lurking in our mind? Then when they finally walk in the room, it's like a cage full of butterflies have been let loose in our stomach and we can't contain ourselves. At just one glance we're weak at the knees and a smile has us shaking all over. Still, can you pinpoint what it is about them that makes you feel this way... What set that sudden spark off in the emotive depths of your brain that made you attracted to them? Maybe, it was their eyes, their smile, the way they hold themselves or a cool gesture they do with their hands, or a quirky expression. You don't know what it is about them, they just have that, "je ne sais quoi;" and whatever that is, you can't get the thought of it out of your head. It's been bugging you for weeks, months, maybe even years!

Sometimes our mind works in reverse and we are repelled by them at first until we realize that what it is; is an unfamiliar attraction to them. On the other hand, you might try to push their attraction away because you're afraid of getting hurt by them, or you see it as a bad idea. The fact of the matter is, there's nothing that really controls love and the ways it chooses to work, it's got a mind of its own. We don't choose to fall in love with someone. Instead, our emotions react to people or experiences that we have with people, which ignites a romantic desire within us, almost like a thirst. We don't choose to get thirsty, we just get thirsty. Therefore, whoever it is, and however wrong it is, you're not getting away that easy. Once your mind latches onto someone it's hard to break free from their bind. Your love is blind to anything but them, no matter how unhealthy it might be for you; you still persevere till you have them as a prize. Sometimes the unreachable is exactly what attracts us to them. We like a challenge and we will drive to all limits to reach our goal. However, the chase is lost when you give yourself away too quickly.

1.2. Tips for finding your ideal partner

"Actions speak louder than words"
(Abraham Lincoln, 1856)

Now as we're on the subject of challenges, which is often our destiny as humans to instinctively search for one! Then, we are also faced with another difficulty, which is getting to grips with the language of love. This is very often missed because we get confused, as we start to think in words and spoken language. We might associate Paris as being the city of love, but we're not going to learn French and bluntly tell someone we have feelings for them. However, great our desire to do so, if we do we're not going to get the reaction we want. It often has the reverse effect. How many of you dated a guy who asked you out after he swore his undying love to you? Similarly, did you ever get turned down because you said too much at the start?

The language of love doesn't speak with words, it has more effect and meaning with actions. When we have feelings for someone, then it sparks an emotion in us, which instantly shows in our body language. Words follow after. When you are too blunt and honest with someone, or simply just state fact with "I like you," or "do you want to go on a date with me?" Then, it is often without success. The best results are obtained by reading someone's body language and utilizing yours to maximum effect. Sometimes this involves actively controlling your instinctive reactions that are driven by your emotions and inspired by heightened passion.

Here is just a handful of ways to make yourself more seductive with body language:

➢ **Eye contact** - Latch on to them with an irresistible sexy stare.

➢ **Smile** - It is infectious!... And a great way to get them to notice you.

➢ **Touch his hand** - make it discreet, but flirty at the same time.

➢ **Stand tall**- When you want to stand out in the crowd, then a tall proud posture is key and enhanced in a pair of heels for that extra 'knock 'em dead' factor!

➢ **Keep an invisible barrier up-** Again don't be too confident, or too forward. Let them reach into you, rather than the other way round.

➢ **Act timid but not insecure-** This is a talent worth mastering! Every guy is secretly attracted to the shy good girl, who can be cunningly confident at times.

Therefore, put all these helpful body mannerisms into place, you've certainly got him within your reach. However, after all that… how do you know, if he's actually that into you? Again, he's probably not going to just say it out loud, if only it were that simple. Instead, he's going to show you the only way he knows how… through his body gestures!

So again here are 10 tell-tale signs to start reading in their body language to be sure that you are onto the right track:

1. **They play with their hands** - it's a sign they are nervous around you

2. **He looks at you intently** - if you catch him staring, then his mind is only thinking one thing

3. **They tilt their body towards you** - it's like their whole magnetic pole is directed at you

4. **He begins to mimic you** - we're biologically programmed to copy each other's gestures, so if we enjoy someone else's company we will start to act like them

5. **Uncontrollable leg movement** - they seem on edge all the time, but don't be quick to think he's uncomfortable around in a negative way - he could be nervous

6. **They smile at you** - if they're happy to be around you they will show you

7. **They frequent where you hang out** - his reappearance will only be trying to tell you one thing, that he has you in his sights

8. **They raise their eyebrows at you** - like you've appeared out of nowhere to delight their senses

9. **His face flushes** - nothing can control it when blood rushes to your cheeks because you feel shy around someone

10. **His pupils dilate** - it's a sign that shows their feeling of ecstasy when they look into your eyes [soul]

So there you have it if he's not yours by now, then he definitely will be soon. Still, how do you really know, if he is the right guy for you...

Now let's go back over a century ago, to 1856, when Abraham Lincoln first voiced the phrase: "actions speak louder than words," which reiterates that what you do has a stronger impact on people, than what you say. We have discovered this with our helpful tips at finding the right guy. However, it has more meaning in the game of love than you think because as well as inspiring thought towards finding the right person. It also allows you to reconsider whether, or not you are in the right relationship, or if you are getting what you really want, or need out of the relationship you are already in. What happens a few months down the line, when the chasing is over and things start to get serious?

Someone might be quick to say 'I love you,' all the time, but are they showing you enough attention, or giving you enough of their time. Instead, do you find they are always quick to pass off on an excuse like: "I'm busy," or "I've got to work?" The truth is, if they really wanted to see you or spend time with you, then they will go to the effort and make that time. So then, you find yourself giving them the ultimatum, and guess what?... They are straight out the door! You are left feeling heartbroken and confused because you took what they said literally.

However, if they weren't showing you enough attention, or they're quick to leave you at the first sign of an issue. Then, these actions are telling you quite the contrary, aren't they?

I wouldn't beat yourself up about it either, because this 'type,' comes under the collected group of men (or women), that are afraid to commit. It could be that they are very full-on in the beginning, but then all of a sudden they lose interest. It is often when the challenge goes and things start to become comfortable or for them- uncomfortable. Do not think that you are the only one who has suffered from their unwillingness to commit:- where you feel like you're 'stepping on eggshells,' every time you try and confront them, or try to take your relationship to the next level! You may just have to accept that sometimes things aren't always meant to be, and you are better off without the heartache. A healthy relationship can be determined in the first few months of getting to know someone, so be wise and make a quick, clean break if you are suffering, before things even get serious.

On the other hand, we might let someone slip from our reach, who does genuinely care for us because we don't pick up on their signs, or worse, we choose to reject them. Why is this?... Is it because we always expect to hear the words spoken to us, or we're expecting charm, to win us over; but does it get us the right results? It's like we are blindfolded by a false hope to tame the impossible when we could be staring at someone who cares for us all along. We're not attracted to this though, are we? We are attracted to the challenge! However, we don't realize that this challenge is unhealthy for us, and often harms us in more ways than one. Instead, we look past the right attention, which is being shown to us sometimes on a day to day basis, often because we are attracted to the wrong 'type,' so then rather than choosing someone healthy for us, we purposely look for people who treat us poorly and make us feel negative about ourselves. Again, this is something I will be looking deeper into later in this book. However, as we're still at first base, then let's not get ahead of ourselves. This is our next rule to finding your dream guy: don't expect it and don't try too hard, or look too far down the line when you think you might have had it. In other words, keep it cool!

1.3. Don't get ahead of the game

"All good thing's come to those who wait"
(Lady Mary Montgomerie Curie, 1843-1905)

Too many of us get ahead of ourselves when we fall in love. Especially, when our emotions rise out of control, from just a small sensation of passion. However, the important thing, if you want to keep your target in sight: is to act cool at all times. Let us take a look at the famous quote used by Lady Mary Montgomerie Curie, a famous English poet who went under the pseudonym of Violet Fane in her poem she titled: "Tout vient a qui sait ettendre," which is a direct translation of the quote in French, although the poem was still written in English. However, in this short, simple saying lies some very helpful advice, which can be looked at from a variety of perspectives. First of all, do not hope too much for love because it will come when you least expect it. Although, it is quite an easy pattern to fall into, when we break up with someone, to find ourselves searching straight away for the next love in our lives. We find ourselves, either hung up on our last love or running at 200km/hr full-speed into the next toxic relationship we can find. We are willing to give ourselves up to the first person we find reasonably attractive, or charming and we're away and gone in the first fish pool we've dipped our feet into, without a chance to properly test the waters and catch the right fish! Then we get down-hearted when we're falling down the same path and hit right back at rock bottom when it all goes wrong again.

On the other hand, we might find it hard to catch a fish at all because we try or look too hard for it. It is important to take a step back and not wish too much for something, then appear from nowhere. It seems a bit unintelligible, but it's an age-old philosophy that if we hope too much for something, then it will never be fulfilled. Instead, as Marie Curie intends to define with her famous lyrical quote: 'if people are persistent and patient, they will finally achieve their goal.' Therefore, an equal balance of patient persistence; or persistent patience will get you your dream guy for sure. Try not to be too full-on, especially at the beginning, but also throughout the early stages of getting to know each other. It should be a slow and easy adaptation, where you learn about each other, not only the good features but also your boundaries. This will be the testing point for you both to learn to accept and tolerate the bad times, as well as the good ones.

However, when you come to win them over at the beginning, then you don't want to give away too much. You have to leave them guessing: 'what will come next.' Make yourself somewhat of a challenge for them. However, there is a fine line to making yourself the challenge and playing hard to get, as well as putting off the wrong image. Do not forget you are teasing them; not playing games with them. They may like to play: 'catch the bait,' but once they are ready to settle in and you're still running the field, they will start to get tired and move onto the next challenge. You especially don't want him to get the impression you are interested in other men, or that you are willing to fall into bed with the first guy you see. Always, make sure you are also giving off the right image from this point of view.

It is important to a guy to know that you are the only one for him if you want a long term relationship with someone. A guy will always put out on the first few dates because they're a complete stud if they do. However, for women, it is the opposite case. When a woman gives in too quickly and lets a man get to the second or third base before the match has even started... Do not be surprised if he stops answering your calls or texts, after a short while. You should let him work at each stage like he's meeting a challenge. Once this has disappeared, then it becomes much harder to keep their attention going. You are also giving them the impression that you would give it up for just about any guy that comes along. Therefore, the longer you make him wait for you, the more he will want you in the long run.

Don't ever let him see you flirting with other guys either; unless you are there to playfully entice him at the start. They want to know you are theirs and only theirs. You should be able to judge the moment when you have won them over without giving too much away, then you are ready to show them the real you. Always remember that the right guy will look for: LOVE, STABILITY, TRUST & AFFECTION... just like you! You may not have found him yet, but "there's more than meets the eye" on this subject. Maybe, you're not looking in the right places or approaching the right people in the right way.

1.4. When it all goes wrong too quickly

"There's more to someone than what meets the eye"

It's an awful feeling when we've tried so hard to win someone over and in just a short amount of time, it's all over. It was all roses and flowers, romantic walks in the parks until a few setbacks turn into an even bigger catastrophe. Before you know it, they're running full speed away from you. Should we ask ourselves if maybe, there was a reason for it... Were you a bit full-on with him, when you could have slowed the gear down? Even a guy who is really into you will feel threatened when you start controlling where he goes or who he sees to soon, at all even. Remember that time and adaptation go hand in hand and can take years to develop. Some of the healthiest relationships develop this way. So try not to get too far ahead of yourself with your headlights on full glare.

However, say you do play too keen, then don't give up hope just yet! You won him over once and you can do it again if you feel like you didn't get a chance to show him the real you; then take the opportunity to do so. You might have had a lot on your mind or you felt confused about your feelings towards him, so you've given him the wrong image instead. Then once he's gone and out of your reach, he becomes a challenge. So how do you go about winning him back?

Take a look at these helpful suggestions I have mapped out for you here and you could find yourself back on track with a man who might seem to have lost interest in you. The more tips you try to cover, the better the chance you have in getting him back. Another good tactic is to try not to go back on yourself, as soon as you give in to your emotions and break one of these 10 rules to getting your guy back then you could run the risk of losing them for good! So listen and act carefully:

1. **Forget him** - It might seem impossible at first, yet it is fundamental to winning back their interest. I know it is easier said than done. It will also take a whole lot of will power. However, once you have mastered this first step then the rest will be a breeze. You cannot send him one million and one messages because it will only push him away. Give him the impression you have forgotten

about him too and it will make him curious. When you find this too hard a task to comply with - delete his number or block him! You don't want to find yourself fatally drunk calling him on your next night out.

2. **Give up drinking your sorrows away** - It is easy to fall into a pattern where you're going out clubbing all the time. You would rather party than stay at home alone. However, a girl who is out drinking or clubbing all the time gives men the wrong impression about you. It can also have negative effects on both your physical and mental health. It can appear to be good therapy during the healing process when getting over someone. After a while, it has the opposite effect on your image and health. It's alright to have a blowout now and then, but not ten!

3. **Join the gym** - Don't take offense to this suggestion or feel self-conscious that you lost your guy because you are out of shape. Alternatively, the 'keep fit plan' is an instant turn on, if ever there was one! It is also a great distraction at keeping your mind free of him, for a while. Furthermore, it attempts to fulfill Step 1: to try and forget him, as well. Now go and get the gym gear out or buy some if you need to. Then get a good fitness regime going and start to tone those thighs and bum because when you're in shape, no man can resist you!

4. **Love yourself!**- Confidence is the key to gaining what you desire! I will broaden more on this topic next chapter, but for now, you are simply learning how to love yourself again. That is where all your love begins. Do you think you can attract a guy without giving love to yourself first? Unfortunately, without enough love inside you, then you will find it hard to attract any love around you. When you are unsure or hard on yourself, then others will follow your train of thought. Once you start to believe that you are powerful and desirable, then people will start to believe it too. It is a simple fact of reflection, which we find so hard to portray.

5. **Focus on your future career**- This is another great distraction and it should also be at the top of your list because you are the most important person in your life; you come first! You might have received a knockback, but this can be a great push for you to focus on your dreams and personal goals. Now there is no one holding you back. Have a think where you are standing in your job and career at the moment... can you reach any higher? It is time to put your thinking cap on and attempt to reach the sky is your limit! Go out and get the promotion or dream job you have always wished for because it will be an excellent confidence booster.

6. **Spiritual meditation** - Meditation is the perfect remedy for relaxing your mind and attracting positive thoughts. When you feel like times are getting tough

and you can't erase him out of your mind. Instead, try and practice erasing everything out of your mind. Buddhists swear by its therapeutic remedies as a way of cleansing the mind and spirit from any bad thoughts. It is natural for humans to become bitter and angry after a heartbreak or two. It becomes our defense mechanism, which we use to protect ourselves. However, it also has a self-destructive effect. You may start to attract an overflow of negative thoughts, which you find it hard to release from. Meditation is one of the most healthy and effective ways to escape from this. It also attracts positive vibes, which should attract more positive energy and luck. You may choose to meditate in the following ways: running, exercising, dancing, painting, yoga, or sitting in a relaxing spot surrounded by nature. For example, you could sit by the sea or in a forest, where you can connect with the natural sounds and vibrations of Mother Earth- an excellent remedy if ever I knew one!

7. **Find a hobby** - Another healthy way to disconnect from your number one prime objective is to find a hobby. Don't forget that the more distraction you can find, then the easier it will become to get over him. It is a hard theory to believe but it is 100% proven to be true! Once you repel your subject, then inevitably you attract them back in the end. Another advantage of finding a hobby is that you are exploring something

you are passionate about, which is a positive step towards building your confidence. It is like building your career but instead, focusing on leisure time. It is a chance to meet new people and make new friends. Think about what you've been missing out on all this time, maybe a sport like tennis or swimming, climbing; a style of dance like salsa, line-dancing, samba or belly-dancing. Whatever it is that you think you might take an interest in, do it! It is good to get passionate about something other than men for a while. You will start to see 'love' in a whole new positive light.

8. **Pretend not to care** - You need to show him that you can live without him by going out and enjoying yourself. You won't get anywhere weeping over spilled milk. So, forget the nights in with a box of tissues. Take some time to ring up your friends, put on a new outfit and go for a night out on the town! Take some photos with genuine smiles and upload them to Instagram or Facebook for everyone to see. Show him that you don't need him, he needs you instead. Besides, where were you before he walked on the scene? Fine and fantastic!

9. **Look irresistible at all times** - It is time to shake off that: 'I don't care about myself look!' Let's face that it doesn't work anymore. It is easy to feel sorry for yourself and let go a bit. However, it will also not work at winning your guy back, or any for that matter. Therefore, when you think the time is right, then go

and freshen up! You can get a new hair do, a pedicure or a manicure, a face-peel; you can also treat yourself to a new outfit or two. Then you are ready, set and dressed to impress!

10. **Forget him completely** - Sometimes the challenge is too hard to match! When nothing else works, then it could be time to '*throw away the sponge*' and start afresh! You have tried everything you can to get him back, but he's still not budging an inch. Then, I'm afraid he's just not the one for you. Sometimes, when he's forgotten about you, then maybe you should forget him too. You don't want to hover around where you're not wanted. Not to worry though, there are 'plenty more fish in the sea,' so let's go fishing! This time search for someone who appreciates you for being you, but also doesn't want to change or lose you at all.

There we go, folks! You have a selection of helpful tips to get your dream guy back, or maybe even, win him over in the first place. Don't get too tied up with the idea because if it is meant to be, then he is sure to be back for more. Once you put into practice one, or more, of these useful tactics you're sure to get his interest back. However, you need to remember that you are not doing all of this just for him. Do it for yourself and gain back some confidence, as well as gaining back some respect for yourself. It is important to not let go of your self-esteem, or start doubting yourself because he's not your prize at the end of the day. You are simply not made for each other. There is a population of over 9 billion people to this day! You are sure to find your Mr. Darcy lurking around the corner soon, just keep these helpful tips up your sleeve for future reference.

1.5. Confidence is key

"Beauty begins the moment you decide to be yourself"
(Coco Chanel)

That's right Ladies confidence is the key and as the beautiful and inspirational fashion designer Coco Chanel once said, "beauty begins the moment you decide to be yourself." In other words, you've got to believe in yourself to make it work. We live in an extremely complex world with the pressures of everyday life, as well as traumas that lie hidden deep underneath the surface. Everything can work at messing with our emotions. Not only this, but they can also have a long-lasting effect on our beliefs, which then turns into a lack of love, and then disbelief in ourselves. Over time, this might lead to more serious health matters, such as anxiety and depression, as well as drug abuse. A further epidemic on the rise at present is suicide deriving from a deep engrained depression. Depression can develop for a variety of reasons. However, it has been connected with trauma from past relationships. Do you remember falling head over heels in love with someone?... Only to find yourself a few days later, flying down the hill headfirst and crashing into Jack and Jill at the bottom. That beautiful fairytale you imagined with 'Mr. Right,' turns into an awful moral tale of: *I told you so!* Your only destiny is to tumble down to the ground with a loud, hard bang!

Then again, you may find the grains running a little deeper. Normally, in a heartache that arises from a personal matter growing up. Mental and physical abuse can have destructive effects on the mind, which controls our body and emotions, as well as our beliefs. When we receive emotive stimuli that stems from a shocking or traumatic experience, then we will instantly imprint it in our memory. It forms a cognitive bubble that protects us from these past experiences. It could be that the very thought of falling in love or getting intimate with someone may seem difficult and traumatic. Therefore, you choose to push them away before you get a chance to know them. Consequently, you could fall into a pattern of victimization where you're always falling for the wrong guy. This is disastrous because you can completely lose your self-worth. You may find it hard to cope with everyday life and relationships, even friendships and connections with family members could become a challenge. It will reach a point where everything will feel like it's breaking apart. The negative 'aura' that has been produced around you from negative reactions, as a result of your negative past will attract more negative energy, which pushes away positive energy overall. In other words, you become completely engulfed in negativity where it feels like everything you touch will break or go wrong. You could find yourself stuck in the wrong crowd or living an unhealthy lifestyle, which is harmful to you in more ways than one. What is more, you may find yourself attracted to the 'wrong' sort of guy; time and time again. We keep falling into a pattern of victimization, which can effectively attract the 'predators' from the shark pool, rather than the nice tame schools of fish swimming on the surface. We don't choose to go for them because they're not on our level, which is down below in the shallows of the deep blue sea with the sharks and freakish creatures that prowl the sea bed.

Remember, life all comes down to quantum physics at the end or day, which is a complicated subject to start looking into. However, when you put it in simple terms, then our solar system stays in orbit based on the principles of magnetic energy. In other words, energy and magnetic vibrations propel everything and everyone we come into contact with. In other words:

POSITIVE FREQUENCY = POSITIVE REACTION = POSITIVE RESULTS
NEGATIVE FREQUENCY = NEGATIVE REACTION = NEGATIVE RESULTS

I will be coming back to the issue of victimization in 'Chapter 5. Why do we fall for the wrong guy?... Where I will explore the reasons why we are attracted to the 'wrong' type. We cannot deny that most women share the awful flaw of being attracted to a 'bad man. What we shouldn't have or can't have makes us want it more, am I right? There are reasons for this unintelligible but very true theory, which we will look at in more detail a little later. However, our focus now is targeted at getting back your confidence, which is more important if you want to see things positively go your way. As the wonderful Coco Chanel intended to say, 'love and positivity comes from within, rather than the other way round.' When we emanate positive energy and vibes, then we attract that energy back. It works like that and no other way. When we give off bad energy, then we associate with people that give off bad energy. Consequently, bad things will happen and they do! This is what we call 'The Domino Effect' because when you line up a string of dominos and balance them standing up; then you go and flick the first domino in line. It has a knock-on effect bringing the next one crashing down into the next, and the next, and the next.... There is no end until you make the change!

This change comes when you get your confidence back and learn to love yourself again. You will have to reverse those nasty beliefs you've built up about yourself because you matter! It could be that *"we only get one shot in life and we must live life to the fullest."* In other words, you must *"take the opportunity, whilst you can,"* and live your life like no other because there is so much opportunity out there that cannot be missed! When you start to look at life like this, then you are on the right path to making a positive and all-important change in your life. I also guarantee you will start to see some more positive results. After that, you can start looking at boosting your confidence by implementing the right tools to your daily regime, which will effectively change your way of thinking.

These tools are easy to come by and do not need much investment. Most of them are down to simple posture and willpower. Then once you know them, all you need to do is try them and comply with them on a day to day basis. You can try one, two, maybe three ways, or even all eight. This chapter focuses on one subject and that is you! It will be the boost to your confidence you are looking for, which will guarantee you supreme 'stardom.' I am going to help you put yourself back into the limelight for everyone else to see just how bright you can shine, how talented and special you are! You are the number one star on this 'red carpet,' and it's not because of how extravagantly beautiful your outfit is or how good your hair looks. You are blossoming with confidence and proud to be the beautiful and amazing you that you are; no one else in the world matters! So be it and for all the right reasons that you will find all heads are turned facing you because of the absolute positive 'aura' that you give off walking in the room.

Does this sound like a familiar, secret desire of yours? Maybe, you see it in other people's lives and envy them for it. Everything they do seems to go their way. They have the dream job, the perfect boyfriend; their friends and life seem glorious, full of hope, and fortunate destiny. However, it could also be that you have taken enough time focusing on everyone else's good fortune, which has left you bitter towards everything including them. You witness an ideal life you see in theirs but can't seem to achieve for yourself. This can spark jealousy within us. Rule number one: never get bitter or jealous of anyone else having a more beneficial life than you. It will never get you closer to your objective, which is 'happiness;' in fact, it will only drive you further away. You have to ignore the distractions around you and focus on bettering your life. Learn from other people who you feel lead a happy life. Follow their tactics. Get to know them and make friends with them. Get to know people who do not bring you down or influence you in the wrong way.

You might also find it helpful to consider at least one of these *"8 helpful ways to boost your confidence in 10 days."* Make sure you keep up with them every day for optimum results:

1. **Be yourself** - Like Coco Chanel once said, *"Beauty begins the moment you decide to be yourself."* You are who you are; who you were and who you will always choose to be, which should be you. The most important person in your world is you! Always remember love comes from within you, so then, when you can learn to love yourself; love is sure to come your way.

2. **Stand taller** - Your posture can say everything about you. You can give off loads of confidence by holding yourself upright and standing as tall as you possibly can.

You've got to stop slouching your shoulders because it shows you've given up the 'ghost,' and all your energy is pointing down. You want it to point upwards for all the world to see so strap on those high shoes and strut your best walk. Love the way you walk!

3. **Self-esteem building videos and audios** - You can find some great videos and audios on Youtube or Spotify that are intended to build your self-esteem using positive - "I can do this!"- phraseology. It will encourage you through intense and energetic repetition that wills you to follow toe, building up the rhythm with a slow intensity that results in you literally screaming the words to the rooftops for all the world to hear. Do not be afraid to do this; it is extremely healthy and you'll certainly intimidate the neighbours if no-one else! This task is especially recommended for you to do in the morning, and also before you go for a big interview to get over the nerves of intimidation.

4. **Look at yourself in the mirror and love your reflection** - When you wake up in the morning and you go take a shower don't be afraid to look at yourself in the mirror and study your reflection with all the time in the world. However, you have to love what you see! When you find yourself looking at your reflection in the mirror next, then stand there and say five or more things that you love about yourself. Be sure to select the right qualities and don't be afraid to change them.

Repeat this task over until it becomes a habit. You're not being vain, you are simply learning to love yourself.

5. **Find a life coach (online)** - Don't think you're the only one who feels a little insecure. There are thousands if not millions of people like you in the world who are feeling a little unsure of themselves, right now. When you find there's something in excess, an issue, for example. Then, you usually find someone who will search for a solution. Once you find it, people will be there to supply the solution, normally with a price. However, a life coach is certainly money well spent! They give you one-on-one coaching on how to build your confidence using helpful tasks and ideas that you can implement in your everyday lifestyle. They will checkup and give you feedback via phone calls, email, as well as, WhatsApp messenger.

6. **Start the gym or find a hobby** - An excellent way to build your ego is by improving your physique. This can be done in a million and one different ways. It is an excellent healthy past-time to distract yourself from any underlying insecurities. You can join the gym or go for a run, you can begin dancing classes or start a new hobby or sport where you will meet new people. A hobby is an excellent way of finding something you are good at and then excel at it with your ultimate mindful-willingness psychology. It is a way of improving a defined version of you. Then you can also build a new

circle of friends who enjoy the same interests, which is another way of boosting your confidence.

7. **Boost your career** - A boost to your career is a boost to your ego! When all else fails and the present is looking a little bleak, you know you can always find a bright future ahead by boosting yourself. It could be time to focus on your career goals instead. Have you been wasting too much time thinking about guys?... Also, where has it got you?... nowhere! Go out and apply for that job you have dreamed of for so long. Attempt a shot at your job promotion because it is time to focus on your dreams. You will see after that, all your dreams will follow 'en suite.'

8. **Surround yourself with good friends** - Always surround yourself with good people. Those that share positive beliefs, but also make you feel good about yourself. Eliminate all the people that bring you down, no matter how long you've known them for. For that reason, you could be getting such bad luck. Negative people breed negative vibes, which breed negative luck and an overall gloomy look on life. You are not out to prove yourself to anyone. When people don't appreciate you for who you are, then brush them off your shoulder and start again. You might find it hard, impossible sometimes. Habit is a destructive thing, and so are people. You might know them well, you might have known them for years. You might even feel that

you depend on them to feel loved, but this is never healthy. Friendship should feel natural with someone who shares your beliefs and appreciates your time, as well as bring out the best in you. When you feel like you are on the lonely road to destruction, then you have to take a break and get away quick! When you socialize in the right places, you are sure to find the right people to call friends.

So then, Ladies, it is time to stand tall and hold up your head high, take a look in the mirror and tell yourself just how much you love yourself. You can practice using one of the most motivating and self-esteem building videos you can find on Youtube. You should do whatever it takes to get that self-esteem back because no one else will do it for you. I know it's easier said than done because slipping back into old habits always seems the more comforting option. However, it is just your mind afraid of the unknown, even when the unknown is a better option for you. It's one of the biggest complexities to the human brain known to man and comes from our evolutionary development that has for millennia depended on a survival instinct. Our evolutionary DNA plays tricks on our minds as we try to adapt to the modern-day world. I will also broaden on this later in the book. What you will always have to remember though is life is short. You do not want to reach old age and think you could have lived your life, differently. The truth is, you can; now is the time! You've got to brush up, pick yourself up, and never let down your pride; not for one second because don't forget... those sharks are ready to pounce!

1.6. What if they're taken

"Would you turn the other cheek?"
(Matthew 5:38, the Bible)

Then there will come that awful scenario that Alanis Morissette paints in her smash hit Indie rock song from the 90s - *Ironic:*

"It's meeting the man of my dreams

And then meeting his beautiful wife"

Now that would be ironic would it not? Then again, maybe you've had this very feeling before yourself. You caught the eye of a new, 'hot' guy in town, or maybe in the office and he's perfect for you. He's well-toned, smart, intelligent, kind and bubbly. What is more... he's drop-dead gorgeous! So, on the next staff dinner, you then meet his equally 'beautiful wife.' The floor feels like it's lifting from beneath your feet, at least you wish it would, in case they see your heartfelt reaction of disappointment. What would you do then, 'you turn the other cheek?' Instead, do you decide to become enemy number one? When is it acceptable to try and win over someone else's guy? Well, let's say it never it is, but if there were a chance... Well, there are a few ground rules.

First of all, you can't go throwing yourself at him at the first opportunity you get when she is not around. That is completely unacceptable behavior. You have to judge the situation wisely. First and foremost is it worth it? At the end of the day, this guy is only a crush, which will pass, especially if he has a family with a wife and kids. In situations like these, I would advise not to take the risk for the destructive consequences that will follow, but also the guilt that you will have to carry with you when all the romance blows over.

However, in the off chance, he is taken and all these options are crossed off the list. Furthermore, it looks like your 'dream guy' has a, not so, 'dreamy' relationship with his present girlfriend. Then it could be you are next in line if you play your cards right. Make sure you stay cool and collected at all times. Play each move with a classy edge towards your goal and don't let your instincts get the better of you. Keep in mind these all-important seven tips I am about to tell you - how you could go about winning 'your' guy over when his relationship is on the verge of breaking up:

1. **Look outstanding at all times** - When you are trying to catch someone's attention, even when it's innocent; you are always allowed to dress and impress. Allow him to compare, whilst showing him what he is missing. Keep your wardrobe kitted up at all times with hot, flattering outfits and take a bit extra time to do yourself up in the morning. Don't let the opportunity go amiss!

2. **Do your research** - To see you have a shot at this guy you've got to find out all the facts first. Do all the necessary research and ask all the right questions. Make sure you have a shot at being his girl before you go in for the kill! Get to know your competition and be sure to find out where their weak spots lie, so you can plan out your strategy carefully. Ask him casual questions about her and do not overdo it. You know you are in for a winner if he finds it difficult to talk about her.

3. **Fill in the gaps... don't compete!** - Once you have found out where their woman goes wrong; it is time for you to fill in the gaps. Don't see it as a competition or try and get ahead of the game. Never be aggressive; instead, be as nice as possible when you see his 'damsel.' Discretion is the key to gaining your prize in this case. Never give yourself away or show that you like him too much.

4. **Give him compliments** - When the time is right, you should drop him a compliment or two. There is no harm in hinting discreetly that his appearance appeals to you. Never give your game away, yet a comment that innocently highlights their look will never go amiss. A remark, such as: "I like your tie," or "your hair looks good today." A woman in a comfortable relationship sometimes fails to give their man enough praise. So after so long, when they hear it from another woman,

it is only going to ring the alarm bells and remind him what it is he's missing.

5. **Console him** - When he's had an argument with his girlfriend and he looks preoccupied and upset. Make sure you are the first to console him and offer him a shoulder to cry on. You don't need to be too forward, just be there to listen to him vent on you a little about his issues with 'enemy number one.' Let him know there is a silver lining if anything goes wrong.

6. **Wait for him to make the move** - Neve be too forward or the one to make the first move. Consider the fact he is taken and you have a reputation to protect, which is more important than a one-off moment of passion with Mr. Drop-Dead 'G.' Take things slow and be patient because you don't want to appear as the *'home-wrecker'.* A little harmless flirting may go a long way, especially if he is attracted to you. I guarantee it won't be long before he comes round. Use a few other tactics I've mentioned here to gain his attention and watch with time, all will have its effect on fulfilling your destiny. When it is meant to be, then it's meant to be. However, when you see there is no chance, let go as soon as you can, to save getting too attached to the idea.

Be the first in line - When you start to see that things are reaching a breaking point; do not let him out of your sight. This is your moment! Make sure you stay simmering in the background and never approach him too quickly. However, always make sure you are first in line when it all comes to an end. He will be looking for consolation and a shoulder to cry on. Make sure it is yours and be the first person he rings when he needs to release tension.

So there you have it, even if your dream guy is taken. Again, there is always hope around the corner. Only, make sure you asses the situation well and never get ahead of your game! As soon as you do, you run the risk of losing an opportunity with him, as well as your reputation. I don't think any guy is worth losing your image. Don't be quick to forget that people are quick to judge, as well as spread the news. Gossip is what drives social exchange, and you certainly do not want to be the topic of negative gossip. It will affect your life, friendships and relationships. Furthermore, it heavily affects your future and mental stability, so protect your image at all times. Never make the first move or a move too soon. When you see that the ice is ready to crack, then you can take your skates and ride over to pick up him out of the frozen fish pool!

Chapter 2

THE HONEYMOON PERIOD

N ow we are getting past the first date stage and we are taking the relationship to the next level. What makes a relationship work past the first date, or even past the honeymoon stage? We all know that if the first date goes well and you're seeing him again at the weekend, then things have gone well. Before you know it, you cannot get enough of each other and every day seems brighter than the last. You have caught yourself singing in the shower at the top of your voice, you see everything in a positive light and your smile is infectious. You are blossoming in love and it's all down to this new guy you have been seeing. You just can't get enough of each other! When you're not together laughing and cuddling, socializing and getting to know his new friends. Then you are sending cheeky messages to one another, via phone messenger.

Nothing can get you down during your 'honeymoon period,' not even a bit of bad news. You're capable of anything and everything and you've never felt so confident. It is all down to the attention you have been getting, as well as the amazing feeling of excitement from the adrenaline that has been rising during the preliminary stages of your relationship. It has been given the term 'honeymoon period,' which means exactly how it sounds. We are not saying you should get married in a few months, it is advised you don't. It will take a few years to live with someone, so you can see that they are the person for you to spend your life with. People are never who they make out to be, especially in the first few months. They put a cloak over their *'real'* persona, which works at luring you in. You are still unfamiliar with each other and making an effort to win the other over. Therefore, if you manage to control yourself and show him only the highlights to your character. It will take time for you to get comfortable together. However, when you do start to feel comfortable with someone, then you will start to *"show your true colors"* to each other. Only then are your 'real' characters set free, to see if a 'real' match can be made.

In other words, don't go walking down the aisle with him just yet. You have to see you can stand the test of time first. Wait for the comfortable stage to follow the wonderful and leisurely holiday period together where you are discovering each other, in more ways than one. In most cases the physical side is explored first where you find yourselves, "at it like rabbits!" The lovemaking is amazing and will give you a new lease of life and energy, unlike any other.

T.S.Elliot was a famous author during the early 20th century who wrote a ground-breaking novel called *Lady Chatterley's Lover.* In this novel he theorizes that *sex* is extremely therapeutic to the body and mind of a human being. He proposes that the natural release of tension in the energetic connection between two bodies making love is essential to our health and mental well-being. In *Lady Chatterley's Lover* physical love is absent in Constance's (or Lady Chatterley's) relationship with Clifford. He is her impotent, disabled husband who was left badly injured after World War I. Consequently, years down the line Constance is left feeling like "vaguely she knew she was out of connection, she had lost touch with the substantial and vital world." Clearly, without physical love in her life, Constance has not only lost connection with herself, but with the rest of the world. Therefore, *sex* makes life worth living as T.S. Elliot puts so spiritually in his revolutionary novel, *Lady Chatterley's Lover*.

However, it doesn't always determine a relationship; it will only complete it. You need to be able to get along and work together as a team through a crisis, as well as your moment of glory. This will be the real determining factor, which will stand the test of time. In other words, when things go wrong, are they going to stand by your side? Now let us take a look at all the ways that you can make, or break a relationship, which is ready in the making...

2. 1. When it all goes wrong

"It's sad but it's true"

()

Okay, so let's start with the worst-case scenario, then we can move on positively from there. You are at a crossroads in a few months, maybe even years down the line. At this point, you should be able to see if you can go left or right, or straight on. Let's consider that straight on - is a definite yes! In which case, things are going really well! All was perfect from the start and the spark that ignited you both together has only got stronger with time. Then again, say you need to turn right, which means you're still on the right path. Still, there is some testing to be done. You are hoping to find that sidetrack that leads you back into a straight forward direction, which is sure to happen. However for now, you have not made up your mind yet, maybe because he finds it hard to open up to you. Don't worry there is still time. Then again, if you are leaning towards the left turn it means that you are in the wrong direction altogether. Everything has gone wrong in the last few months and you are not even at that serious stage, yet. In other words, you will have to face the lonely road to nowhere. Okay, maybe not as bad as this, but you will have to accept there is no future with you and this guy. It is time to find someone more in tune with your radio station.

We cannot deny that falling in love is, beyond belief sometimes, one of the most amazing feelings in the world. On the reverse spectrum, falling out of love is the ugliest sentiment to be haunted with. We go from delighting ourselves in the most intense, ecstatic and passionate emotions with our partner in crime, to hitting a brick wall! Therefore, love can most definitely be a crime, especially in this case. It is a crime to make us feel so high one minute and so low the next. Then *when it all goes wrong* you are engulfed in a whirlwind storm of sorrow and despair. There is only one word to fit the description- your worst nightmare! Even worse, you often have to suffer a little before it's all over, as you watch your relationship fall apart. In general, men find it hard to voice their feelings. Instead, they might decide to communicate their *true* feelings through their body language with manners and gestures intended to hint that something is wrong. You might start to read these signs, but then you are also afraid to lose him. This leaves you stuck in an awful '*no man's land*,' where no one says anything; yet the problem still keeps progressing and getting worse, which essentially makes you feel more insecure about your relationship. It can also result in you questioning yourself at times too. All the while, you will try and communicate with him to get a reaction off him, which could push him further away. So, then you give him an ultimatum, but don't be surprised that you might have to push the subject forward, just ask him: "Where is our relationship going?"

I would not expect red roses and a box of chocolates because if you've started to notice these tell-tale signs when your relationship hasn't had the opportunity to reach the 'real' serious stage yet, then it could be that he takes the opportunity to tell you, what you've been dreading to hear. Prepare yourself for the worst! However, I am going to help you to get ahead of your game. Here are some helpful tips to check up on, whether or not the hourglass is reaching its final grain of sand without the hope of turning back the other way:

➢ He stops calling you

➢ He stops answering your calls

➢ He replies to your messages late, or never

➢ He doesn't look at you anymore

➢ You catch him looking at other women

➢ He ignores you when you are talking to him

➢ He interrupts you with something completely off the subject that you are talking about

➢ He makes excuses not to see you

➢ He makes excuses not to have sex

➢ He is less affectionate to you

➢ He is attentive before sex and then loses interest afterward

➢ He avoids the places where you frequent

- He criticizes you all the time

- He tries to suggest ways for you to change your look

- They sigh heavily when they're around you

- They let off bad energy around you

So, if any of these signs are familiar to you, or maybe even multiple ones, then rest assured you could be coming to an end in your relationship. You cannot let it destroy you! Look at the bright side, there is better to come. When you have reached this stage you are suffering, often without knowing. You start realizing these signs and already your doubting yourself, beyond belief. Then your belief becomes ridden with doubt.

2.2. Make it work

"It's all or nothing"
(Billy Holiday, 1958)

So, how do we make it work then…

Well, there are a few tactics! All these guidelines and rules might mean it is hard to relax in love. However, to follow the spider's complex web, then you need to keep within its intricate, so it can lead you to the center. Never get stuck because you'll be eaten by the wicked spider. Always be ahead of the game like the female spider, who eats the male when she has finished *procreation*. You do not have to follow this concept literally, but certainly play men at their own game. Be sure to put the right tactics into practice and with cunning, careful persistence you will win his affection.

The aim of the game: stay cool at all times! It was rule number one when you came to winning him over and it is rule number one to holding them firmly in your grasp. Do not overpower him with jealousy, but also avoid over-messaging him when he is busy or having timeout with his friends. Irreversibly, you are sending him the wrong message. Instead, play the *'hard-to-get card,'* now and again. You want them to want you, as much as you want them. To do this you must not show your feelings at first sight because it might scare him away. You have to appear to keep a healthy balance of emotions. In other words, you like each other, but you cannot like each other too much because one will over-balance the other. For women it is proven to be harder to keep their emotions at bay at this stage. We might be able to keep our cool at the start because we are put off by the over-intensive behavior displayed by our male counterparts. Until we fall for their charms, then it is all downhill from there.

This is all down to you! Love is what you make of it. When you lay the tracks pointing downwards, it will go down; lead them upwards and the will go up. You are in control of your destiny, both in and out of love with someone. The only trouble is now you have to consider someone else is involved in this equation, your man. Men display their emotions differently when they are in love. When they reach their goal, which the first stage is getting you to bed with them, then they start to relax. It is not that they don't want more with you, than this. However, their needs become different. Where you might have flirted with a guy once to get the other's attention, then when you have the *right* guy it's time to let your flirty side go.

As the saying goes, *'it is all or nothing,'* which believe it or not, is true here. Firstly, in military terms, it is "a method used for armoring battleships," which is ironic because you will have to travel over a whole sea of other fish and sharks until you find the right man. Then when you have found him you will have to shield yourself in sheets of strong armor to reach the finish line. In other words, if this is a relationship to last then forget all the other men, no matter how charming they are because you have your man already. When you are caught talking or flirting with other men, which he sees or hears about; you won't be giving a good image of yourself. Expect to receive a clean cross across your door, even if a bit of flirting got you there in the first place. You might find it difficult to let go of the single-life yet, but then you decided to take things seriously with someone. Well I'm afraid *'you cannot bake a cake and eat it all on your own now,'* you have someone else's feelings to consider in the matter. Therefore, if you are not ready, but then feel completely distraught when he walks out the door. You can only imagine how you would feel in his shoes if the same happened to you, so what do you expect?

Therefore, when you start to behave like this in a relationship, be sure that you have lost your man in 10 days in the following 10 ways:

1. **When you start to nag and moan at him all the time** - save your desire for a good *'vent'* for your girlfriends because they are the only ones that are going to give you the right advice from a woman's point of view. Men will shy away from most women's problems, as well as their own, which we will get back to later.

2. **When women cry** - Similarly, when women openly show their emotions clearly and erratically, it will scare a man away. They would rather shut out their problems and put on a brave face. In other words they have a much more relaxed outlook on life. When they see a woman cry they will feel awkward and not as affectionate towards them, but only because they're not in tune with our emotional reaction to a crisis. Therefore, it is better to put a brave face on and save the tears for a *'once in a while'* occasion.

3. **When women drink** - This doesn't mean that you cannot have a drink, now and then, when you're out socializing together or with friends. When I say a *'woman who drinks,'* then I mean a woman who is a *'drinker.'* Therefore, a woman who drinks *too* regularly or reaches a drunken state to a point where she cannot walk anymore, but her beloved has to carry her home.

Although it is sweet in the beginning, it could come to a quick close before the next weekend *'binge'* is up. Before you know it, he running the field again, whilst he leaves you behind in the gutter. Alcohol can help you release your inhibitions, especially if you are feeling shy around him. However, you must not pass the line and let your inhibitions go completely. Even when you are borderline drunk, you are not so attractive to him anymore. Learn your limits with alcohol because it is key to guaranteeing a long term relationship.

4. **When women lie** - Did you feel the need to make up another image of yourself to impress him? Were you covering up a night out or when you secretly met up with your ex? Whichever the scenario it was; however taboo the subject was to talk about... It could be that you don't want to give yourself up and you don't want him to find out something he might find offensive. However, he will find it more offensive if, and when, he finds out in the end. Every relationship should be built on trust. Therefore, if you can't share the truth with him, then the chances are you are not sure about him anyway. Take the time to see if you are willing to commit to the man you are dating before you are ready to take your relationship to the next level. You do not want to fall into the path of the twisted wheel of karma's fortune. We all know that *"What comes around goes around."*

5. **When women accuse them of cheating** - When your emotions start to grow stronger for someone, then they can start to spiral out of control. During the first stages of the *'honeymoon period,'* the heated passion during sexual intercourse ignites strong emotions that connect you and your man on a deep, spiritual level. However, this can spark natural jealousy in a woman who wants to protect the status of their man, as theirs. The very thought of her man sharing a bed with another woman could start to haunt them, even eat her alive with jealousy. When your mind starts playing tricks on you, say he is talking to another woman, and she is pretty. Then it triggers the alarm bells of jealousy because this woman is presenting you with a threat. It could be that she does have ulterior motives, yet it is up to you to take control of the situation. However, this doesn't mean pounce and go in for the kill. Instead, learn to control these jealous emotions because they are unattractive, especially when he eyes only for you. Be proud that this amazing guy who others find attractive is yours. Trust him. Do not make the mistake and accuse him of cheating when he's completely devoted to you. After a while, his devotion towards you will slip if you pursue the thought that he is being unfaithful to you. He will tire of your accusations and before you know it - he's gone! He will leave you and be in the arms of someone else, so essentially you are wishing it upon yourself.

Learn to let go of your insecurities and be careful what you wish for, but also what you say and how you act around him when other women are on the scene. Words next to actions play the second most important role in our complicated game called love. They can make or break a relationship all the same.

6. **When women overpower men** - A woman who comes across as too extrovert or needy, they run the risk of chasing a man away. Remember rule number one - you must always keep it cool! It will pay for you to control and calculate your emotions correctly, depending on your guy's reactions, which you'll discover with time. You have to find the balance and never steer too far overboard, or he'll jump off! You want to give him a challenge and keep him reaching to that challenge, which is you. Never give yourself away too quickly. Let him discover the *'right'* you and not the intense, *'crazy in love'* you. That first person he fell for, but who he also wants to be with. Let him believe that he has won you as a prize by making him work and put the extra bit of effort in to keep you satisfied.

7. **When women flirt with other guys** - A guy is attracted to a girl for a lot of reasons and physical attraction is one, maybe a harmful bit of flirting with someone could win them over and show them what they're missing. However, when things start to get serious between you, but he still sees you flirting with

other guys; rest assured he's not going to stay interested in you for much longer. Therefore, it is time for you to decide, whether or not you are serious about this guy or not. When you are serious about someone, then you stop flirting with other guys.

8. **When women go out a lot** - When you become adapted to a certain lifestyle, then it is hard to adapt to something completely different. For example, when you adapt to having a partner after being single for so long. Once upon a time, you were free to go out and do as you pleased. You could stay out till all hours of the morning if you wanted to because you were your own master. However, when you commit to someone in a relationship, then you have to let some of these liberties go, like going out with your friends every weekend. You are still your own person, but you're sharing your time with another person. You have to accept his boundaries, as well as feelings. Would you like it if he was always making other plans to go out clubbing? Would it seem like he is still living the single life and not showing enough commitment to you? A man is quick to get the hint if you are putting off an image that you want to stay single, even if you don't feel that way; be sure you are not acting that way.

9. **Women that are too argumentative** - Men do not mind a woman who can speak up for themselves. They may even be attracted to it, as long as that opinion is

shared by them as well. A woman who is too quick to jump to an argument and give her opinion, especially if she's always out to shoot a man's theory down will come across as a definite threat to a guy. When you display this kind of attitude, then you will soon lose their interest, as well as respect. Men might be easygoing most of the time, but they are also proud, dominant creatures who will feel threatened by a woman who is always out to argue their point of view.

10. **Women that are too deep at the beginning** - When you get too deep in the first few months, you run the risk of driving him in the opposite direction. You have to take slow steps at the beginning for his reassurance, as well as his own. Win over his trust before you start exposing your deepest secrets too him. It could be that he's all over you sometimes, especially before he has got you into bed with him. Do not confuse this and start offloading everything that has ever happened or gone wrong in your life. Personal secrets are meant to be shared with time and getting to know someone properly, not just in the bedroom. It is important not to share too much personal information with him at the start before you have a chance to get to know him. You never know when he walks out the door, and if the relationship turns bitter, then he may use this information against you. You do not want the whole hood to know where you are from.

When you start to display any of the following characteristics around a guy and you wonder why men are always quick to run a mile after a few weeks, or months; well, now you know why. The reason is that you have exposed one or more of the following behaviors around him. Then it is also guaranteed, that he will or has already left you. Whenever you are quick to say that it is them all the time, but then you find these signs familiar. You should start to wonder if it is you, and not them, that could be you driving your man away. I understand that it is not easy to know how to react, especially when some reactions are out of your biological control. However, to move your relationship to the next level you will have to put in the effort, as well. This will include taking the time to keep your control, keep them interested, but also play your cards right. When you start to have feelings for someone, then try not to go full pelt at them with a gun full of emotions. Alternatively, you should slow down a gear or two, so that you can take the time to learn about the person you have such strong feelings for. Furthermore, be calculated and cool with your approach to him and make him feel like he has a prize to win, which is you. Therefore, as your feelings start to get stronger, you should learn how to control them and not to give them away so quickly.

Have you ever been seeing for someone for a short amount of time, yet the passion that is aroused during sexual intercourse with him has driven you to say *"I love you"* out loud? However, when you've been seeing each other for just a few months, then how can you love him already? When you barely know him. The erotic and passionate emotions that are aroused during sex fuel adrenalin that feeds this feeling, which we confuse and often define to be love. It is not, for example, the same love you will have for your child or a partner you've shared your whole life with; your sister, or your father. These are much more dependant and stronger bonds of love that you create with someone who you've known for much longer, yet why are we driven to say this? Well, there is a secret, which I'm going to let you in on later. The Ancient Greeks thought up a revolutionary theory millennia ago about love. It is impossible to believe that this theory, most of us are unaware of, has been around for thousands of years, but it has.

2.3. When it works

"We're walking on sunshine and it's time to feel good"

Now let's look on the bright side, where say, you do play your cards right, then months down the line you are even more in love. You are on a straight road track to a successful relationship. You have found your amazing *'dream'* guy and you have got past the *honeymoon* stage. Life is working in your favor and you feel like singing to the treetops that you are happier than you have felt in a long time. You happy because you are in love. You talk about moving in together or start planning your first-holiday getaway together. This is a great idea because it will bring you even closer together on a much deeper level. Take the chance to explore a new place and culture together in your moment of passionate pleasure. You will be surprised at what you might discover about each other. More importantly, make the most out of this moment in your relationship because it is the beautiful stage of discovery. When you are falling in love your senses are enlightened to every new experience you make together. The first experiences you have together make the framework of your entire relationship, so make them count.

There are ways to know when you have won their heart over, and you are not just another notch on their bedpost. Unfortunately, some men are not so quick to say goodbye when they have lost interest, especially when he hasn't been presented with a better option. Therefore, if you see that he is unwilling to commit to you, it might be because he's not that sure about you. However, he still craves sexual satisfaction, which you give him. This is a cruel scenario to find yourself in, but it happens to the best of us. I would not be too cut about it, if you have found yourself in this situation, then make sure it was only once and not twice, or even more. Move on and find yourself someone who appreciates you for being the wonderful person you are. Someone who also wants to spend time with you and not let out of his sight. You can't be suited to everyone, maybe at the beginning, you will be. Few people connect on a deeper level because only selective people are meant to know the *real* you. Otherwise, there would be nothing special in that person who is *really* meant for you. He may have presented you with a challenge, which kept you coming back for more. However, a man who hasn't shown you respect up until now, never will. You are worth much better than a late-night booty call at the end of a night. He might finish the night off with you, but it is only for one thing.

Women who get wrapped up in romances like these will find themselves on a long lost road to misery, where they will never get past the first stage of love. They will always find themselves as the second option and not the first. This may be hard to believe, but this is down to people's mental conditioning. In other words, people make their own destiny based on beliefs they have conditioned on themselves. Therefore, a woman who gives herself away to a man too easily is setting herself up to be second best him, not the other way round. It could be that he keeps her within reach, as a *'just in case'* option, until a bigger challenge comes their way. Again, when you find yourself in this 'catch 22' scenario, then you have to break out quickly. Once is enough, but falling into a pattern of dead-end relationships is unhealthy for you and your mental stability. Love should present a safe and secure partnership, as well as satisfy your dating and sexual needs.

Do you want to know when a guy has really made his mind up and is completely devoted to the idea of making a future with you?...

Take a look at these helpful signs that show when a guy is falling in love with you:

➢ He can't take his eyes off you

➢ He can't keep his hands off you

➢ He is the first to initiate plans

➢ He is always smiling

➢ All his body language cues are directed at you

➢ He allows you to open up and be yourself around him

➢ He is equally himself around you

➢ He pays attention and listens intently to everything you say

➢ He always agrees with you and shares your opinions

➢ He introduces you to his circle of friends

➢ He includes you in his life and leisure time

➢ He is always complimenting you

➢ He starts to act like you and talk the way you do

➢ He starts to propose plans with you

➢ He opens up to on deeply personal matters to you

➤ He cares about your needs and problems and will try and help you

➤ The energy around you both is always positive and there's a strong connection when you are together

When you start to read any of these signs, then you have nothing to worry about because you've got him well under the thumb. However, if the alarm bells are ringing to tell you that he is displaying the very opposite. Well then, you are probably in the category of girls that he sees until he finds the one he wants to introduce to his friends and spend every hour of the day with. However, if you can tick most of these boxes off, then rest assured you are on the right track. Do not let down your guard just yet because if you are happy and things are going well; keep it that way.

When you have something good, then be sure to hold on to it and enjoy every moment like it's your last. Make memories together and adapt to each other's flaws. That way you are sure to create a loving bond between you that others are in awe of. Always remember, none of us are perfect and there will always be tough moments, which are set to test your relationship. These are the moments that prove, whether or not your love is meant to last. You will see whether your man is destined to stand by your side, through thick and thin. It could be that the romance starts to wear out a little after the first few months of passion. Therefore, you might need to start implementing other strategies when you reach the more serious, comfortable stage in your relationship. You may want to start thinking out of the book to keep the excitement going. You might also need tips on how to keep the conversation going or to encourage them to stay passionately attracted to you, which involves getting a little experimental at times in the bedroom. It is an excellent way of bonding and discovering more about each other. Explore your bodies, whilst unraveling your bedroom fantasies to get a deeper insight into one another's minds. Watch how your mind and body properly come alive with the expectation of what will come next.

Chapter 3

STANDING THE TEST OF TIME

So we are now past the honeymoon stage and we are well into the comfort zone... phew! Now it is not a reason to run a mile, just because the romance doesn't seem, as strong as it once was. He may not buy you flowers or even take you out to dinner as much, which can sometimes make you feel like he doesn't show you the same attention. It may even hint to some of you that he is falling out of love with you. However, this is not the case, he has never loved you so much. The only trouble is that as men and women, we have very different outlooks on love. We're always working in reverse with each other. Where the man will chase the woman at the start and the woman will remain a little subdued; then the woman becomes attached to the man through sex, which a man will too unless he sees there is no challenge. He may very likely move on then to the next new challenge. Whereas, a woman may let her guards down and throw herself at him, which he will immediately repel.

Once we get to the honeymoon stage there is a wonderful peace where two minds and souls meet in perfect and passionate harmony. When the harmony is upset, then usually one or the other is very quick to break the seal before they get too attached, which effectively causes the other to portray stronger feelings. Again, this is because they are in the losing position. However, say that the serene harmony carries things on to the next level, which is what we call the serious and comfortable stage in a relationship. Here you will get the chance to discover the *real* life-partner that you have chosen for yourself. You learn to grow in love together. Life is now a journey, or a challenge even, that you will take on board together. It will put you under a whole load of pressure and stress that you will now have to tackle together. This can be a challenge in itself because first, you have to get to know one another properly. You must also find out each other's flaws before you can move on to the next stage. Only then can you see, whether or not your relationship will stand the test of time.

3.1. Time for adaptation

"It is not the strongest of the species that survives, nor the most intelligent. It is the one that is most adaptable to change"
(Charles Darwin)

When you get comfortable in a relationship with someone, then you know you can depend on that person. However, we have to come back to the pure basics. First of all, the character traits that connected you at the beginning, which brought you to the more serious, 'stable' stage in your relationship overshadow your differences. Only until, they start to become exposed and clash with each other when you start to disagree.

With every good trait comes a flaw, which we work hard at hiding when we are unfamiliar with someone, especially if we want to gain their undivided attention. However, when we become comfortable around someone we are more prone to expose our *'true colors'* to them.

You may find some character clashes derive from gender differences, as well as expectations that each person has of the other. Men can provide excellent support and are even better life partners, when they're not irritable, which is another characteristic that starts to show after a while when things get comfortable. When couples are more open to displaying signs of mood changes that they once resisted showing to one another. That is when we start to notice flaws in each other and characteristics that annoy us sometimes. It can also be caused by spending a considerable amount of time around each other, sometimes too much time. When you find this happening, then take some time out from another. You can catch up with your girlfriends or spend some time with your family. Just do anything you can to disconnect from one another for a while. When you come to meet again at the end of the day, then you will appreciate each other after spending some time apart. This does not mean you have to take a break in your relationship. You must not think erratically at the first sign of something going wrong. I would not believe that the grass is greener on the other side. Instead, maybe you just need to wait for your garden to blossom and grow. You can add some more water if you need to and allow some more sunlight in, then wait. Always, expect the odd storm, which might kick up one or two flower beds. Then make sure you get back to work to give them some TLC after the storm has blown over. You are sure to get your garden looking beautiful again.

This is what many of us forget about love. That it is, in fact, a necessary adaptation between two people. The first intense stage, which is full of glorious expectation gradually wears away because you get to know the person that you feel so strongly for. The strong emotion, which arises out of sex may pass a little. However, this cannot be mistaken for true love. In reverse, a love that remains hooked on a passionate sexual relationship is short-lived and unstable. When you reach stability in love, which is slightly more relaxed, rather than less exciting. Well then, you know you can depend on this person for everything. When you look at the whole spectrum of possibilities that is to come in your serious relationship from today onwards, which could include discovery, progression, marriage, buying your first house, kids. Then, of course, watching them grow side by side and ending your lives together retired in a wonderful holiday home. Imagine somewhere with a hot climate where you are sipping on Pina Coladas ending your evening looking out to the sunset holding hands. It could be that you imagine this life for yourself, as a silver lining, or perfection that you will never reach. However, it is yours for the taking when you can learn to adapt to one another, but also adapt together with changes that will happen in your lives.

It might not all go to plan because you might get into debt, or you might also find it hard to juggle work and family life. Life will set out obstacles and pedestals that you will constantly have to cross and climb all the time. However, if you do it holding hands and learn to accept one another's differences, then it is the only way you can survive and reach the top! As Charles Darwin professes with his evolutionary statement that "it is not the strongest of the species that survives, nor the most intelligent. It is the one that is most adaptable to change." Therefore, to keep the garden growing and alive, which is essentially your passion; you will need to put in the extra effort.

After a while, the romance becomes less intense, which is when we feel freer to tell one another how we feel about the other. We may also decide to wind the other up or feel more irritated by each other when we are feeling under pressure or a lot of stress. However, when the passion goes, which inevitably it will, then so will the adrenaline with it. Only because it is not made to last forever. You cannot associate this feeling with a bleak outlook on love, as it is simply a natural progression out of the initial meeting and feeling you get from love. This should then mold into what will become a more steady and stable, but also a healthy relationship.

However, we tend to get confused by the idea of what love is.

I would say, as men and women or as opposite genders, we have different perspectives of love, but also how we show it. I will come back to this theory in the chapter where I will be taking a close look at the theories John Gray raises in his book, *Men are from Mars and Women are from Venus*. He impresses how women desire love to be constantly displayed to them shown through attention, romantic gestures, as well as emotional attachment. Although men, will still become very emotionally attached, they show love differently. A man likes to get physically intimate when he gets deep with you, rather than emotionally. In some cases, men will open up to you, but on rare occasions. They feel more comfortable holding their emotions inside, rather than feel the need to release them. As you can imagine this presents a real clash between men and women, which John Gray brings to light in his revolutionary bestseller, *Men are from Mars and Women are from Venus*.

However, let us now focus on what we need to keep alive, which is the fire burning in your relationship, once it reaches the serious stage. We can adapt and learn what each other's interests are, then we can spend some time sharing and enjoying one another's interests; the opportunities are endless now...

Find out what his style is. How does he enjoy his past-time? What is his favorite hobby? What does he like to watch on television? What is his favorite food? It is time to get to know your man and learn to adapt to his tastes. You should learn to enjoy and love them with him, as well as anticipate his needs. These are just a few tricks to keeping a happy man at home.

3.2. How to keep the love alive

"Engage in things that set your soul on fire"
(Alex Elle)

Now let us take a look a bit further down the line and fast forward another six months to a year later. It depends on every couple and every individual character that determines when the romance will start fizzling out. However, usually when couples get more comfortable with each other or used to the other's company. It could be as a result of spending more time together, as well as factors, which arise when you frequent someone more often, especially in a loving way. For example, when you open up to each other about personal information, but also you start to properly explore and discover one another in the bedroom. Both of these factors are extremely important factors in determining just how serious you are about each other, especially from a man's point of view. It has been tested and proven, although a man has his emotional side and will search for someone they can depend on, as well as bond with sentimentally; a man is attracted to a woman's physique with preference to the legs and bum first. His eyes lead to these before he gets to know and fall in love with a woman's character. A man will also express his love for a woman, primarily during sex. To them sex is love and they require a regular supply of it to feed their cravings, which quite honestly (unless something's wrong), is at least once or twice a day. All the emotional ties that come with a relationship he will fulfill to satisfy a woman's needs so that she will satisfy his, which are much more simple - sex!

However, sex is also an excellent way of keeping the love alive as well, "[engaging] in things that set your soul on fire," therefore, we are going to give preference to our man's favorite leisure time. As, we have discovered that this is what sets a man's 'soul on fire,' then it is his prime language to talk in love. So, why don't you see how he feels about you? Why don't you give him the benefit of the doubt and set the scene for a completely compatible and physical explosion? When you start to see things get a little tired at home, then pump it up a notch. Do you find that he has not been giving you much attention recently? It might be a good idea to instigate the attention first...

So when the mood is right and it's a Friday night, you have the whole weekend ahead of you. How about, you set the mood with a romantic candlelit dinner and a bottle of wine to let down your guards with some sexy underwear and a full-body makeover. Make sure he gets the hint, of course, in case he decides to go out for drinks after work. Send him a cheeky text, or a phone call. You could even whisper it in his ear before he goes to work in the morning, "make sure you come home straight after work, honey. I've got a surprise in store for you." Give him a sexy smile and a wink. I would expect him to run through the front door at least an hour early with an extra bottle of wine in his hand, as well as an extra-large smile. Then, when you decide to finish dinner and it is time for the *real* bonding time to start, switch off the lights and take some time out in the bedroom with no technological distractions. Turn off the phones and televisions; laptops and tablets because it is just you and him and a fresh set of sheets to ruffle up. Have fun together and set that flame aglow with an everlasting flicker of love and passion.

Therefore, in light of this it could be more helpful to know what pleases a man in the bedroom, then you are sure to rock his senses wild! So sit tight and take careful note with these 10 ways how to satisfy your man's sexual needs quickly and successfully:

1. **Cut to the chase** - forget the foreplay and get straight to last base

2. **Surprise him** - whether it is a new place, or a new position or idea, even just surprising him with sex when he is least expecting. To a man surprise inspires him to be instantly turned on.

3. **Lots of affection** - women are not the only ones who like a cuddle, a kiss, or a caress on the cheek; men also crave female affection during sex.

4. **Domination** - Men like to dominate in the bedroom because it is their chance to let their natural male instinct loose, which will involve taking dominant positions, as well as letting their energy go by releasing their complete bodily power over you.

5. **Relaxation** - An equal balance of intense love-making with more relaxed moments of pleasure will seriously set his soul on fire. Get the essential oils going and create some sensual deep heat to arouse his nerves and sensitive spots.

6. **Morning sex** - Men wake up in the morning feeling naturally aroused, it is a fact. Their mind is in a state of relaxation, which sends natural signals to arouse their area of pleasure, essentially feeding it with a fresh supply of oxygen and blood. So oxygenate him some more!

7. **Oral sex** - Whether you like it or not, we know they do! Get him to drink fresh pineapple juice and you will notice a definite sweeter, more pleasurable taste

8. **Fulfill his fantasies** - Find out his ultimate sexual fantasy, and as willing, as you are to fulfill it, then you can at least try and meet him halfway.

9. **Anytime / Anywhere** - As you know, men are highly aroused and will be up for it anytime and anywhere. Therefore, find the opportunity to slip away when you are out together for some cheeky alone time; it will bring you both to an instant climax!

10. **Likes you to climax** - Men will not be completely satisfied unless they know you are too. When a woman climaxes, then it arouses an instant urge of passionate gratification in a man, which essentially helps him to release, as well.

3.3. Anticipate his needs

"Hi honey, I'm home"

Men have a strong, physical, and sometimes dominant appearance about them, which hides the fact that a man needs looking after. It all rests in the *'Nature-Nurture theory'* where women were born to take care and mother the children and men secretly crave their mother's attention. A sentiment or craving, which becomes lost as men grow into full-grown adults, but never leaves them. Therefore, you often in a single guy who lives alone misses the female care and attention, as well as the support he used to get from his mom growing from a boy to a teenager. They find it hard to keep up a tidy home or keep on top of the washing. Maybe even everyday survival instincts like eating properly might become a chore that they are unfamiliar with. They have always had everything served to them on a plate, then if they also witnessed the rest of the family, like their fathers, sisters and brothers get taken care of at home by the one and only super mom, what do you expect?

In a way, many men are conditioned to believe that women should take care of them, which most women will fulfill because they have an instinct to follow suit - called a mother's instinct. Of course, men can look after themselves they can find it easier dealing with a crisis sometimes, where women might panic. However, it is a fact that most men when allowed the chance, enjoy to kick back and relax on the sofa, whilst a woman potters about cooking and clean around them, generally taking care of the household. It will give them an inner gratification like no other! However, in our modern world, women have quite rightly started to become more independent, as well as take on equally, or sometimes more demanding jobs than their men. Therefore, they have become more disinclined to continue their role, as 'mother hen.'

Then again, when you are ready to succumb to waiting on your man, now and again, well they are sure to love you all the more for it. You might just have ticked that final box by providing them with a secure and caring home environment to raise a family in. This very simple fact, is all men look for in a relationship after sex, physique, and the perfect character match. It determines the final decision for them that you are not just a girlfriend, but a wifey and maybe the mother of his children one day. Therefore, when you are ready to put the effort in to show your man that you can provide this for him and see him standing proudly by your side, then it's time to start anticipating his needs and looking after him a little more. You're not his mother, you are simply taking care of him because he is yours: "to love and to cherish till death do [you] part," as far as the wedding vows will take you if that is what you wish for with this one. He will also take care of you and make you feel secure in different ways; you just have to learn how to read them.

When you are ready to settle and take the time to tend to his needs, as well as learn how to anticipate them. Then, you are also ready to stand in prime position as the number one woman in his life. Therefore, you may decide to:

➤ Cook him his favorite food

➤ Prepare him a packed lunch

➤ Wash and iron his shirts

➤ Tailor his wardrobe

➤ Give him constant affection and reassurance

➤ Look after him when he feels poorly

➤ Preoccupy yourself about his personal life

➤ Encourage him in his career goals

➤ Give him helpful advice

- Take interest in his interests

- Give him space at times

- Learn to read his body language

- Anticipate his needs before he gets the chance to

- Be the host when he invites friends round

It might seem like a pretty hard job description, at first sight. It might also get monotonous after a while. At times you may feel a man is too dependent on you, then you have almost lost your independence. Once upon a time, a woman didn't have the opportunity to work as they do today, whether they liked it or not, their job was to look after the household. However, in the last 70 years women have gained their independence back with a world full of opportunity and high hopes. It has led to great social change, as well as an overall desire in the modern-day woman to prove herself, especially in the work-place and with her career goals. Although modern-day women will succumb to their position as the carer of the household, they now look for more support from a man than there ever did before to carry out certain household chores. It is only natural for you a woman to feel bitter after a while when she does not get the support she needs.

A woman who works a high pressured job and gets home to a house full of screaming children, but then has to cook everyone dinner, whilst her dear husband kicks back with a beer comfortably watching the T.V. Well, she is sure to reach her limits soon enough. It may take weeks, months, even years; however, her mind is slowly simmering and reaching a boiling point deep within her veins, which is ready to blow the kitchen sink open if a change is not made to her life soon. A woman mustn't reach this surplus of emotional anxiety because it is unhealthy. Therefore, before you reach this boiling point talk to your man. Don't let him override that you are suffering at home without enough help tackling everyday tasks you can share. Try to communicate with him in the right way that you need some help without getting too frustrated and aggressive on the subject. This will not aid the situation; it will only instigate an argument.

In other words, it is not a reason for you to fly off the wall and raise the rooftops! Unfortunately, a relevant characteristic, which resides in women due to monthly hormone changes, which can heighten erratic emotions and mood swings when we find it hard to cope with the everyday 'obstacles,' or pressures life can sometimes present. Again, men are not in tune with these hormonal changes or mood swings. Therefore, they find it hard to get to grips and understand women in these moments of necessary monthly *'discharge'* of heightened emotions. He may also react negatively, especially when he's adapting to your mood changes, so it's always good to keep your cool and take it easy on him! Remember that all-important rule that got you here in the first place. Well it will also keep your relationship going strong and guarantee its ultimate success. So, take a deep breath and count to 10, then do it all again! However, when you are ready to voice a change in your household, then don't also be afraid to.

All you have to do is communicate and calmly compromise a change. When you voice something aggressively, then you will only get aggression back or intolerance. Be wise and accurately voice your desires, only like this will you get what you want, one way or another. It may take time and patience, but will it out of you because it will work to getting you closer to your desire - complete satisfaction in love. Never forget this fact now girls, which is that - women can be very powerful, more powerful than men can be when they can learn how to control their emotions and use their god's gifted intelligence:

OBSERVE - ANTICIPATE - ACT

...with absolute cunning discretion!

3.4. Keep the conversation going

'Lost for words…'

You can sometimes find that when a relationship gets too comfortable or maybe you yo have had one, or two clashes, or disputes, then it can be hard to get the conversation going again. It isn't always easy to put your emotions into words.

Women are open to expressing their feelings and emotions, whereas men may choose to bottle up their feelings or intercept them in another way. They find it hard to express their feelings, or they might not voice them at all, which is sometimes a little incomprehensible to the female mind; and so it goes on.

However hard it seems, it is still essential to find the right level of communication. In the early 17th century, an African-American preacher enslaved in the state of Virginia led a revolutionary rebellion as an attempt to abolish slavery and regain the civil rights of thousands of African-American slaves. During his time, he did not succeed, yet his speeches and rebellion took effect in the overall attempt to win back the people's freedom. One of his wise statements read that:

"Good communication is the bridge between confusion and clarity."

In other words, if you want to voice to your man that you are unhappy about your relationship, then do so the right way. When you feel like you are doing too much or you could do with some more support. Then, it is time for you to communicate this to him and start-up that all-essential, life-changing conversation. It could all be up to you to provide the conversation breaker; still, that is fine because you are in control of where it goes. Therefore, if you want to talk about the plans you have at the weekend, or you want to make plans. Maybe, you want to find out what's on his mind because he's preoccupied, or you might also want to find out more about him. Well then, it is up to you to present him with that all-important question.

This could be any of the following:

REASSURANCE:

1. *"What is it you love about me the most?"* - Is it your smile, your eyes, your huggable thighs... Maybe, it's the way you roll your eyes when you laugh! Find out and feel rest assured there will be at least one, if not many things, that will set his heart alight every time he looks at you.

2. *"If you could change anything about me, what would it be?"* - None of us are perfect, but maybe there is a feature about you that offends him and you wish to find out what it is. We cannot change one another, but we can learn to understand what it is that annoys each other.

3. *"Do you like me better natural or with makeup?"* - Women naturally like to play dress up. The fact is, a woman's image is becoming more and more important in a society, which is breeding a sort of 'selfie' vanity in a lot of people. However, 99% of guys will always say they prefer a woman stripped bare and confident to wear a face with no makeup. So go on then, give your skin a rest and make his day too!

HOW WELL DO YOU KNOW EACH OTHER:

1. *"What is our favorite romantic spot?"* - It all started somewhere, that 'spark', which sent both of your heartbeats racing when you looked into each other's eyes. Maybe, you looked at one another so many times but never like that before; and never in the same way again. You realize that you are in love and it all happened somewhere. You probably find yourself revisiting the spot together to remind each other of that glorious moment, which brought you together as one.

2. *"If you could go anywhere, where would it be"* - We all have a dream place we wish to go to! You should make each other's dreams come true and share the memories. Make plans to visit the places you both desire to visit more than anywhere else in the world. You are ideally talking about making the most of your leisure time together.

3. *"What is your favorite food?"* - All men have a favorite 'comfort' food. Well, let's face it - we all do! Get to know each other's tastes and homemade specialties. Take time to treat each other to your ultimate culinary surprise, which bakes some great loving therapy.

SPACE FOR IMPROVEMENT:

1. *"Do you think we could improve on our love?... if so, how?"* - It could be that you are living the dream and

there is nothing imperfect to your relationship. However, this is very often not the case. To reach perfection, you have to work at it, which takes time and lots of effort. Find out how you can improve on your love together.

2. *"What makes our love different from all the rest?"* - There has got to be something that sets you apart from all the rest. Whenever you are together, you set the world aglow with the love that you share for one another. Take time to glorify this fact and talk about what makes your love stand out over other relationships around you.

3. *"If there was anything I could do for you or you could do for me, what would it be?"* - There is always space for improvement in every relationship in love. Those who say there is not and believe their love to be perfect are sure to find a flaw hiding under the surface. It usually needs lifting through communication. Therefore, always suggest ways you can compromise and help one another to become a better pact; an unbreakable one.

10 YEARS DOWN THE LINE:

1. *"What shall we have for dinner?"* - It is that all-important moment in the day, that still 10 years down the line remains your favorite time when you can sit down and enjoy a meal in the beautiful company of

your beloved. Spice it up then! Don't order a take-out tonight, or cook him just another average meal. Ignite the love back into your relationship with a candlelit meal for two. Try something new from the cookbook to alleviate the monotony from your everyday usual cuisine.

2. *"How are you feeling?"* - It is a short simple question that shows you care about them. It could be that your guy seems a little on edge or preoccupied, maybe he's absolutely fine and looks happy in love. However, you just want to hear him say it. Rest assured that he will appreciate your attention unless there is something really wrong. Then for some reason, which is still a mystery to women, they say - nothing!

3. *"What are you most afraid of happening to us?"* - How has he been acting around you of late? You are 10 years down the line, yet you hopefully have another 10 years ahead. In which case, make sure you are completely happy in your relationship together to save another 10 years, of what could be, hell if you choose to stay together living unhappily. On the other hand, it is also natural for every couple to get insecure in a relationship, but it should be short-lived and infrequent. A little communication should be able to confront, as well as effectively relieve any insecurities felt by either party. However, if nothing alleviates after all this time, then you might want to start mapping out

your Plan B, which could be making a life-changing decision to go 'solo' and strong, rather than remain insecure in a loveless relationship.

3.5. How to communicate with a man who can't

"All behavior and feelings find their original roots in some form of communication"

Men can be mysterious beings. They can also be hard to read sometimes. One of the characteristics of a man that will strike women the most is a man's inability to communicate his deep inner feelings. All couples need to confront their issues to overcome, or in some cases, heal them. However, women also forget that not all men find it easy to communicate these deep-set thoughts. Some men chose to reflect on deep thought with a cold and collected reaction because it is their instinct to stay strong and protect, rather than show weakness. Therefore, it is not that they do not wish to communicate what haunts them the most, but they biologically feel they shouldn't have to. In other words, they have an inbuilt frame of thinking, which despite their issues or troubles intercepts that they must put on a brave face and carry on.

However, a woman may naturally become preoccupied with a man's inability to communicate his thoughts and feelings. On the contrary, they see it is beneficial to let go of one's built-up tension and emotions by talking. In truth women are right that a troubled man will run the risk of his troubles eating away at him, which could leave him feeling cut-off from everyone, as well as alone and severely depressed. Over the last decade there has been a significant rise in suicide rates by 25%, which leaves the age-adjusted suicide rate in 2018 at 14.2 per 100,000 individuals that die from taking their own life. The numbers exceed by a long way with middle-aged men at the highest rate reaching 70% of all suicide deaths carried out in 2018.

These statistics are very worrying and I give a lot of reasoning to the fact that most men suffer from an inability to communicate what is upsetting them the most sometimes. Once upon a time, men wouldn't have the chance to sit back and daunt on everyday stress and trauma. However, we live in an extremely dependant and modern society that is presenting us with more challenges than we properly take on board. First of all, as a species we developed slowly until modernization and technology went hand in hand flipping our society upside down. Most of us have not been given the chance to adapt to it in a way that we are biologically familiar with yet. Therefore, our bodies and brains find it hard to cope with this new lifestyle that we see changing every day.

Therefore, a man that cannot communicate is simply following his survival instinct, which in effect he doesn't need anymore. Instead, that survival instinct has become something that he needs to work on by communicating how he feels. Therefore, as women who are the 'masters of communication,' it is time to put your skills to the test. You may find yourself living with a man, or even in the company of a man who seems to have something worrying him, but doesn't seem to be able to voice it. Take the time to try and lure it out of him and lure him out of his dark thoughts. It is important not to give up trying to break through to him because he may choose to give up on himself. It could be that another reason, which has affected the rise in suicide rates, may also be down to the equal rise in separated families in the last decade. It could be our man finds it hard to voice his feelings, but whatever you do don't give up trying; give him a chance to slowly come round by implementing one of these helpful tactics:

- **Be patient with him** - do not get anxious and pushy with him when he fails to communicate because it will force deeper into himself. Time and patience is the key to gaining his trust, which will bring him round to opening up to you in no time.

- **Ask the right questions** - Language is a powerful tool when it is used in the right way. It is amazing how the way we choose makes all the difference sometimes. Therefore, word your questions carefully.

- **Find the right time** - Choose the perfect moment to open up a conversation that he would not usually dive into when he is feeling relaxed, or when you are intimate with each other. Ask him gently and reassure him with lots of affection.

➤ **Don't over question him** - If he's not ready to talk don not pressure him. When you ask too many questions, then he is likely to shut off quickly. Find the right time and ask the right questions; keep them short and simple so you can get to the point.

➤ **Crack a light joke** - A little light humor will often get the conversation rolling in a more serious direction because you are easing him in gently and positively.

➤ **Find out what shuts him down** - Learn to judge him and find out what shuts him down. It could be something you said to him or even the way you said it. Maybe, someone else is getting to him. You will never know until you find out what it is that shuts him down.

➤ **Distract him for a while** - When he fails to voice his feelings on a matter, then it is best not to press him about the issue. Turn him off the idea altogether by distracting him and changing the subject, then, when the time is right, come back to it.

➤ **Keep him feeling relaxed** - Reassure a man that they can open up to you by making him feel relaxed about the idea. Do this by giving him gentle affection as he confides in you. Make him realize he can always confide in you.

➤ **Listen and agree** - These two skills are key to getting him to confide in you over and over again. You shouldn't need to voice your opinion because what he needs is for you to listen and reassure him. Always, agree with him, whether you do or not. For now you should be happy that you have finally got him to voice his feelings to you. In other words, you have made excellent progress! You must continue like this for a while before you start to voice any heartfelt opinions, which could run the risk of losing his confidence again.

➤ **Don't bring up the past** - Maybe he has hidden secrets that stand like a barrier between him and all the other people around him, including you. They are almost always hidden in a dark past of pain and trauma that has risen from suffering an unfortunate experience, either in their childhood or with another relationship. The possibilities are endless! However, do not be the one to always bring them up because they are his secrets to share.

There we are, you might have found it hard to communicate with him before, but I'm sure you won't find it so hard now. Take your time and be patient with him and carefully implement these helpful ways to get your man and open up his deep, dark secrets to you. Anything that is bothering him at the moment, then he might choose to share with you if you take each conversation with the right amount of care. Love is a game of compromise, so to make it work; you must sit down and see each other for who you really are. You need to accept that your man finds it hard to communicate and ease information out of him delicately, rather than forcing it out of him aggressively.

All minds work in mysterious ways but are extremely fragile too. We are all susceptible to other people's reactions, therefore an inability to disconnect with you may not mean they don't want to. It could be that his inability to communicate rests in emotions, which lie deeper set than you could ever imagine. They may lie somewhere hidden in a world full of secrets and trauma they wish to escape from, but do not know how to. They could also take more time to resurface, therefore brace yourself. Always remain calm and strong because you are his support. The memories are his and not yours. Therefore, if he trusts you enough to share them with you, then be sure to take a delicate approach to the subject in the future, once you are aware of all the facts. Then be sure to lay them to rest. Try not to bring them up again in conversation unless he chooses to. You have done your duty, which was to allow him to open up and confide in you. Now it is time to focus on your bright future together full of hopes, dreams, and happiness for you both to share in harmony!

It is important to remember that it isn't because they don't want to open up to you but because they don't know how to.

It is up to you to help them find a way! It is your job to work as a team and bread a healthy relationship together adapting to each other's ways. Instead of trying to change one another. Only then can you help one other to become the better you and him working together as a team.

Chapter 4

COMPLICATIONS IN LOVE

Where every relationship can go well and be a match made in heaven; every relationship can also go horrendously wrong. Nothing is ever what it seems. It could be that you turn down Mr. Right for the charming, hot guy that won you over in just one stare, but who also ends up being a complete devil in disguise. He is only out to ruin your hopes and dreams, but some of you won't find this out till your well and truly trapped in his snare. This sort of controlling relationship happens more frequently than most of us choose to believe. Unfortunately, they are only set out to destroy your beliefs! You may start to lose confidence and even love for yourself. Then again, you may get loose from a toxic relationship, but then you are destined to fall for another bad relationship, and another, and another! Here we find ourselves falling into a pattern of victimization, which can be fairly destructive to our overall wellbeing and character. It will leave you feeling bitter and twisted about love when you find yourself always falling in and out of love with the wrong guy. We will touch upon this in the next Chapter. 5 *Why do we fall for the wrong guy?*

However, in this chapter, we are going to look at what happens when complications start to arise in your relationship, or when the love starts to die out. You are left feeling lost and alone in your own home. This is devastating and extremely unhealthy for anyone who feels like a prisoner, or a victim in their own home. It could be that your man is not necessarily aggressive or controlling, but instead he doesn't notice you exist anymore. An unappreciated woman will begin to underappreciate herself, which will start to imbed itself in her beliefs. Soon she will be left with a completely negative opinion of herself, which will start to show in her lifestyle and habits, as well as the people she frequents. She will set herself her line of dominos, then place herself underneath the last one. She will do it without realizing what she is setting herself in for.

To succeed and be happy in life, you must believe in yourself! You must believe you can do better and feel better because every day is a new experience and life is the ultimate challenge, which you will surmount to when you start believing - you can do it! It is natural to feel down and insecure at times, as long as it is only sometimes, not all the time. Life is meant for living, so live it like no other. When you decide to make a change in your life for the better, then you will start to see things more positively. When there is no room for compromise in a relationship, then it is time to look ahead and never backward. In other words, it is time to leave him and get your life back!

4.1. Compromise to make it work

"Compromise is coming together and finding a solution agreeable to both parties,"

If there's one thing you and your partner should do sooner rather than later, it's learn how to compromise in your relationship. This skill can come in handy in a variety of situations, from choosing what to do on vacation, to fixing problems in your sex life. And it means doing it all without arguing, hurting feelings, or pushing each other away. It shows that the relationship itself is more important than being 'right' all of the time or always getting your own way." It also shows you're approaching life as a couple, and one who wants to make decisions together.

A compromise can happen if and when you and your partner don't share the same love language, but still want to make each other feel comfy and cared for in the relationship. To do so, be honest and lay it all out on the table, so you both know what's up. Do you like physical touch? Do they like when you give little gifts? Make an effort to "speak" each other's love languages more often, even if it doesn't come naturally, in order to reach a compromise. This is one of those milestones in a relationship that enables us to grow and evolve as human beings, probably why two parent home is deemed invaluable across all races, culture and ethnicity.

4. 2. When you hit rock bottom

"When the rough get's tough, the tough get's going"

Not every relationship has a happy ending. Many come to an end after so many years, "when the rough get's tough, the tough get's going." Unfortunately, when your partnership has reached the point of no return, which may be a failure. However, rather than watching you both fail with it. It is much wiser to take a step back, shake hands, then walk away with dignity. A loveless relationship or marriage is unhealthy for you both and will only result in resentment, as well as bitterness towards each other. No one wants to be stuck behind four walls with their worst enemy because it would be a living nightmare. You will start to feel like a prisoner in your own home! This should not be the case because your home should be your haven and a place to disconnect from the rest of the world. Life will present its fair share of demands, whether at work or an everyday trip to the supermarket. This in itself is a challenge because say, for example, you are waiting for a parking space and then all of a sudden a great big, brand-spanking-new 4 X 4 pulls in front because you drifted into a daze, wondering where on Earth your life is going right now...

Then when you have to come home to Mr. Misery-Guts, or even worse World War III goes off every time you walk through your front door. The situation is devastating for anyone and least of all should not happen to you. Don't rest in thinking that there is nothing better for you round the corner. No matter where you are in your stage of life, be it your: career, age, dependency, mental well-being...

Be sure to make the break soon because your happiness matters; you don't want to see yourself here in five years feeling like this, or even worse! Everyone is entitled to be happy, and that includes you. You must stop looking at everyone else happy around you wondering why this isn't you. You have been here for so long and where has it go you? Unfortunately, it got you nowhere, but there is still time to make a change. Accept that some people weren't meant to change, but you can! Don't let him change you for the worst when you see a love affair has turned toxic, then it is time to hang up your white flag and surrender. You need to stay true to yourself and the only way is to stay true to your beliefs. Protect them and keep them sacred. Don't ever let a guy make you think you cannot live without him for the wrong reasons.

When you start to feel underappreciated in your relationship, or like your partner isn't fulfilling his side of the bargain properly. Then you begin to see that you are suffering it is time to make a definite change. This may mean giving him an ultimatum. When you see no results there, then it could be time to leave him. It may seem the most impossible, unthinkable idea in the world, but you've got to remember who makes you happy. Is it him? Well he should do, but no it isn't him; it's you. You are the person in control of your happiness and you are the person that controls the situations you put yourself in to arouse happiness, or on the side of the coin - sadness. Therefore, if you stay in a relationship that isn't making you happy, or satisfying you in a way that you feel you could be, then take a break! You have to be brave and hold your head up high; take an empty suitcase; fill it with everything you need, which is just your heart, your head, a change of clothes, toothbrush and ID; then proudly walk out that door.

You will never feel more yourself until you make that all important decision to change your life and work on making it better. You need to move out of the unhappy situation you are in. You also need to start learning how to love yourself again before you go on the hunt for your next number one. A relationship like this will take a while to overcome the heart-felt sorrow, which he has left you feeling. It may appear to be the end of the world, but not when you take the time to discover yourself again. There is no more dark shadow standing over you anymore holding you down. A relationship should not be a dependence on one another. Instead, you should work to help one another become better people through the love that you willingly give to others. I'm not saying it is always going to be white horses and a glamorous carriage to take you off to 'Neverland,' because we are not a fairytale. This is true life and that's why we call it 'Neverland,' because it doesn't exist. We mustn't get confused and expect every relationship to be perfect, either. There will always be ups and downs, which will put our love to the test.

You may find yourself in all sorts of a mess, which often neither of you can help. It is also natural for your emotions to get the better of you and for the heat to rise out of control at times. As long as it is infrequent and short-lived. Then again, an argument can often help you grow as a couple and allow you to confront one another on certain issues that may have been bugging you for some time. As long, as you can lower the tempo quickly, then talk it over and understand one another's reasoning. You have to work at creating a healthier relationship, which will stop this from happening again.

When your relationship reaches this *'rocky'* stage you have to start making wise judgments and decide: is this relationship worth saving or not?

How do you know when to judge this?

You look deep inside your heart and ask yourself these three important questions:

1. Am I happy right now in my relationship?

2. How long have I been unhappy in my relationship?

3. Could I be happier in my relationship?

And if your answers read a little like this:

1. No

2. A long time time

3. Yes

This is when you know you are ready to pick yourself up from *'rock bottom'* and start your climb to the top of the mountain peak where you should see yourself to be. It could be that you only get one life, then you should live it to your absolute maximum potential! No one else is going to live it for you and no one else should be making your decisions for you, either. Make sure you get your independence back and create a happy haven for you to come back to, even if it is just you. Get some peace back in your life and routine, then before you know it you will find yourself a better man. Someone one more in tune with you and appreciates you being in his life. Then you will be left wondering why you didn't make the decision sooner. No need to think like this though, there is no time like now! Take a break and go back to being your own master in the making.

Never become over-shadowed with doubt. Always, be proud to be the amazing person you are and find someone who shares your same beliefs. I can guarantee he is out there somewhere, it just takes time and patience, and a pair of binoculars. Take a sneaky peek and guess what you see? A mass of men for miles to see! So, take the time to select the right one. There's no rush, just because you have lost a few years of your life rushing into a relationship too fast, therefore take a few years to search for the right one and enjoy your freedom for now. You will only ever discover the 'real' you - single and free again!

4.3. When love gets toxic

"Love is blindness"

In the worst-case scenarios, which can happen more than people let other people believe. It is an unfortunate case if ever there was one when a woman finds herself in a relationship, which isn't just unhappy or unhealthy; it's toxic and destructive. Domestic abuse is something that simmers under the surface and has been an epidemic for centuries. In some countries and cultures, and certain social groups it is worse than others. Unfortunately, where it was gradually improving in Western culture from 1950 to the year 2000. In the last decade, we have seen a fluctuating rise in domestic abuse or women who find themselves in an over-controlling relationship with their partner. The reasons for this are a little uncertain. No doubt there is some underlying sociological reason behind it.

Whatever the matter, it is an epidemic that needs addressing much better and more often. Why?...

The reason should be obvious, but when a woman finds herself in this situation, even in a very dangerous position; she is *blind* to it. First of all, she runs the risk of losing her self-control. She is also in danger of being hurt by the man she loves and often lives with, where nobody else can see, in her own home. This is when a woman is no longer a prisoner in her home, but a victim. Furthermore, it can have extremely destructive effects on a woman's physical, as well as mental health. When a man gets physically abusive with a woman, he is so much stronger than she is. He can do more physical damage to her and in some serious cases; a man will kill his woman.

On the other hand, psychological abuse, is just as harmful. When a man takes control of a woman's mind, which they can do with the utmost calculation, gradually easing them into the idea that they are the ones in control of them now. It could take months, if not years down the line before a man starts to display antipathetic signs intended to control and make their woman feel low and underneath them. In the beginning, all seems fine. They may shower you with gifts and compliments to lure you in. To most women the first few months will seem like a normal relationship where nothing is out of the ordinary. It seems hard to believe, but unfortunately, over-dominating men are often intelligent and charming men. However, do not get confused in thinking that all intelligent, charming men are evil monsters! It is just a trait, which runs in controlling, abusive men. It works as a tool to lure in his prey, which is the woman. Then gradually, he will implement his control on her in small doses, to begin with, then when he sees her fully enveloped in his Venus flytrap he will let the snare fall and - snap! This is when the *real* madness starts and he will increase the level of abuse until it reaches the destructive, harmful stage.

Unfortunately, there is a pattern in this scenario as there is with everything. First of all, a man with this character very rarely changes. Second of all, they usually target *'the victim'* type, which will enhance that person's feeling of victimization, if they fall for their trap again. They might successfully turn someone into a victim as well, which makes them male predators. They are often unrecognized because of their charming, intelligent character that works well at manipulating and controlling women to believe their behavior towards them is acceptable, but also that a woman will deserve punishment. Here, she could enter a stage of victimization, which is incredibly hard to get out of because her beliefs have been changed to feel this way. She might even decide to pity her 'predator,' and hope to change him for the better. Furthermore, she may focus only on the good times with the hope of rekindling them, as well as become the hero who 'tamed the beast.' However, there is no fairytale here where Belle is close to reaching her happy ending by counting down the last rose petal. The Beast will not change into that handsome, perfect prince they have been waiting for. Instead, they will be left with an empty stalk and no beauty to share with the right person and live a happy, healthy life with.

There's always time to change those beliefs and the change comes with accepting that this is not the right man for you because you deserve someone who makes you feel good about yourself. Unfortunately, there is no room for change in circumstances like these. You should not have got here in the first place. Although it doesn't matter that you have, as long as you make the change quickly to break free. Do not wait another second for him to gain any more control over you. It is easy to get yourself into a position like this because '*love is blindness,*' and our eyes are clouded by the love that we feel for them, even when they are hurt by him. Then he has her fully wrapped in his snare and dependant on his control. In times like these, family and friends can be very helpful, so do not shut them out. Let them in and help you get yourself back to being you. Stay away from him and you'll soon see that everything he made you believe was only set there to take control over you. However, he does it to protect himself from his own deep insecurities. Remember that you are not there to heal them though, you've tried that and it didn't work. He is never going to change, but he could change you for the worst. Therefore, take the break and run as fast as you can without looking back because no one wants to get themselves in a situation like this.

Chapter 5

WHY DO WOMEN FALL FOR THE WRONG GUY?

Have you ever wondered to yourself *'why do women fall for the wrong guy?'* Maybe, you have considered that there is a pattern or some underlying reason that still baffles women, and men alike. Do you remember that first opportune moment you were presented with those first two boys at high school who both had a crush on you?

One presents himself to you who is the option a) his hair is combed straight to one side, his t-shirt is neatly tucked into his corduroy pants, he wears a giant grin and is holding a bunch of flowers, which he's picked from the hedgerow. He is the most intelligent kid in class and destined for an amazing academic future. Even though, he didn't have the highest number of hits on his friend's list. Then there is option b) Mr. Popular who stands there dressed in a black leather jacket, like Danny Zuko, puffing on a cigarette, in the smash-hit movie Grease (1971). He is looking you up and down like he's going to eat you alive. Therefore, which one did you chose?

Let me guess... Was it option b)?

The only trouble is most women don't know or realize that they are falling into this pattern in love where they find themselves choosing the *wrong* guy all the time. They latch on to a trend without knowing they're doing it. However, when you find yourself in this fatal pattern you have to fall out of it quickly. This is difficult to do, but it is up to you. Everyone has mechanisms to break their negative pattern of behavior, which all stems from training the mind to believe differently to what you have been taught to believe. The belief we need to change is that: Danny Zuko from *Grease* is not the best option for Sandy, who is an intelligent, studious girl with a bright future ahead. The results are shown in the last scene where you see her dressed more provocatively, but also smoking and flirting more.

Sandy's character has completely changed for the worst because she seems more aggressive. However, the movie has chosen to idolize these negative changes in Sandy, which is all the more confusing. Therefore, we wonder is the media slightly responsible for a woman's negative conditioning, which leads many to believe that falling for the wrong guy is cool, after watching this movie? You are about to discover the answers to most of these questions in this chapter where I hope to share with you some pretty juicy secrets. I'm sure you are all desperate to find out: why is it that women choose to fall in love with the wrong guy?

5.1. Falling into a pattern of victimization

"You are a victim of your own mind"
(Jack Kornfield)

One of the reasons we find ourselves falling for the wrong guy is because we've done it so many times before. It starts to become a habit and we follow a sort of 'pattern of victimization.' It is the process of becoming victimized by someone who takes the opportunity to have control over you. After that each shark follows after the next; each one trying to make you feel more of a victim. There is only one direction this will take you and that is soaring downwards. When you find yourself in this mindset, which is all it is. It is a frame of thinking that you have created because you keep falling back into a detrimental pattern of negative relationships that breed negative feelings, and effectively work at destroying you little by little. What is important for you to remember is that you are in control of your life and emotions. It could be that you were once made to feel like a victim, and you didn't see it happening.

However now, you should be able to recognize this behavior and see it in other men. You should become a professional at reading them, so you know when you see them, you must run away. Never get yourself in the position again where you feel like the world is caving in and there is no way out. Whatever you do, don't go back to the *'predator'* type; start searching for the 'right' type. It might take some getting used to at first. You might even need to train your mind to believe that this is the right guy for you, not the '*boring*' type as you have been used to thinking. The fact is, he isn't boring, he's just different; he's good for you. He might not give you the same sudden rush of adrenaline, every time he walks through the door or when you get that call you have been waiting for; after so many weeks or months that he's been gone without a trace! What you don't realize is the expectation is unhealthy for you after a while. You need stability to guarantee happiness.

Therefore, when you are ready to break the pattern; remember that:

YOU ARE NOT THE VICTIM; YOUR EXPERIENCE HAS MADE YOU STRONG, NOT WEAKER!

YOU WILL NOT ALLOW YOURSELF TO FALL FOR THE BAD HABIT OF GETTING INTO BAD RELATIONSHIPS ANYMORE.

THE FUTURE IS YOURS FOR THE TAKING, SO TAKE IT BECAUSE YOU AM NOT A VICTIM ANYMORE!

Always keep this mindset and break out of the destructive pattern of victimization, as soon as you find yourself falling into it. When you are already 70ft under and swimming with the sharks with no apparent escape route, then it might be a good idea to go back and read Chapter 1.5. *Confidence is key*. It will surely give you some tips on winning back some confidence, as well as learning to love yourself again. It is also the key to coming out of the evil snare, which is victimization. As the Buddhist preacher and psychologist John Kornfield once prophesized with his spiritual quote: "you are a victim of your mind." You must stop pointing the finger and blaming everyone else for your misfortunes. You hold the keys to your engine, so make sure you're the one to turn them in the ignition. You are not a culprit but are when you continue to make misfortune for yourself. Therefore, reconsider the next time you put yourself in the position to receive more misfortune from another guy, if not the same guy - he is the 'wrong' guy.

5.2. Always on the hunt for a challenge

"The fascination of shooting as a sport depends almost wholly on whether you are at the right or wrong end of the gun"
(P.G. Wodehouse)

Humans like to rise to a challenge; we meet any obstacle, whether it's too high, or impossible to reach we still won't give up until we've tried. We'll go in for the kill! I guess that is what makes us the top of the food chain, which is our unwillingness to stop at the first pass, or the second, third, even fifth attempt. We want what our hearts most desire, which is usually what it shouldn't. We will never get the message that when the answer is no, it is no! However, did we ever question why the answer is no? Could it be, that we didn't present them with enough of a challenge to satisfy their equal need to meet a challenge? Think to yourself, why is it that you even like a challenge?

Now let's go back to our two options where there was the man holding flowers stood at the door with his shirt tucked too far into his pants. Then again, there is also the hot, slightly disheveled guy at the bar who smiled at you walking in but is now chatting to the barmaid. Who would you find more appealing to you... and why?

Well let's say, the second option is because he presents you with more of a challenge to you, whereas the first *'gentleman'* type, although very sweet, tries too hard and doesn't present you with a challenge. You know that if you invited him in for coffee, then they would jump at the opportunity shaking with delight. However, does not this appear to you as a complete turn-off? So then, imagine if you are putting yourself in that same position. In other words, 'I want you way too much', or 'I am way too desperate,' then it wouldn't be attractive.

Maybe you did present him with a challenge at the beginning and he was all over you, which was then a complete turn-off. Finally you succumb to his charm on the odd occasion of circumstance, maybe a drunken night. However, when you wake up the next morning, then you think "oh god!" However as fate has it, you meet him again and for some unknown reason you find yourself winding up beneath his sheets again. This continues for a while without you showing much interest, you might even decide to date other men. He might have been really into you, which improved when you started seeing each other, but then he's put off by your incoherent attitude. Therefore, he decides to move on to the next challenge because he sees no future with you. However, now he becomes a challenge, so you decide to chase him. Except now, he shows no interest in you anymore, so your left wondering why? But also, a little offended, as you think: why does this keep happening to me?

It is because you decided to chase a little too late. However, love shouldn't be about the chase; it should be about presenting yourself, not necessarily a challenge, but a prize to be won. Feed a man's desire to rise to the challenge, which is you at the finish line. Never give yourself away too easy, but also never be the one to chase a man. You can always have feelings for a guy, but try to win their attention in the right way. To do this successfully you have to control your emotions and feelings of attraction towards him. You have to calculate your every move:

➢ Leave hints that you like him, but never throw yourself at him.

➢ Never make the first move, unless he gives you the opportunity.

➢ Never give in to him on the first date, or the second if possible.

- Feel free to ignore a message or two from him, once in a while.

- Always play it cool as a cat, never let them ahead of your game.

Unfortunately, love is like playing a game sometimes, but only if that is what you make of it. When you start to look at love as a challenge, but that it is yours to be won; expect to receive it. Then implement the right tactics and ensure it with the belief - he's mine! Be sure to hide this thought, as best you can, whilst feeling it. There is a definite chance that he will be yours soon. Then if there's no chance it was because there was little in the first place.

5.3. The Fatal Attraction to the Alpha Male

"We are all ready to be savage in some cause. The difference between a good man and a bad one is the choice of the cause." (Jane Austin)

A woman is attracted to the 'alpha' male who is confident and charming, physically appealing; but also stands out as the pack leader within his large circle of friends. This is the ideal man for a woman, not because he is drop-dead gorgeous and popular. It is because our bodily instinct is attracted to his dominant *persona*. This doesn't just date back a year, decades ago, or even centuries ago. It dates back millennia, to our primal ape species that is deeply ingrained in us. The 'alpha' male leads the pack and the women will follow. He will devour every woman in sight and every man who challenges him won't get a word in edgeways. Therefore, you find that these men who pose as the 'supreme' lover, often date more women than one. They are female predators who will not rest at one woman. Instead, they need many to satisfy their highly strung ego and libido.

The 'alpha' male type is attracted to women who are confident and pretty, but also a little shy and submissive under the surface. To them it presents them with the perfect 'alpha' female partner to stand by their side. More often than not, they will share their bed with other women that fit the same category. However, they will never amount to the same status as their 'alpha' female. What about the 'alpha' female though?... And what about all the other women that follow suit?

When you find yourself a pawn in this biological game of chess or the queen for that matter, then expect yourself in a situation that is destined to end in tears. He may be, especially desirable, yet he is to just about every woman in the room - he loves it too! It's in his nature. Remember that you are never going to be his number one, there will always be another woman or more. Then arises the worst-case scenario where he could start to portray over-dominant behavior towards you, which develops into a toxic relationship; especially, if you're always willing to submit to his charms. Therefore, remain strong when you get a 'whiff' of the 'alpha' male's attention.

This may present you with a more of a 'challenge' because as fate goes, you will present him with the challenge; so expect him to chase you when you say no. I would advise you not to give in to him because you know what is to come. Rest assured, that it is in their blood. They are this way and don't think you are ever going to change them. Once you catch sight of a player, it is much more beneficial if you walk away. That is, only if what you want out of love is happiness? Then be sure to go for the right guy and not the wrong one. All the signs show in his body language. Therefore, is the guy overly charming? Well then, he's probably like that with everyone - he is a serial flirt and cheater!

5.4. Warped by the Media

"The people will believe what the media tells them they believe." (George Orwell)

Now I want to come back to our example of Sandy Olsson in the movie Grease. I want to figure out why they chose to idolize her at the end of the movie as she willingly throws her dreams away at a prosperous future to fall for Danny Zuko's fatal charms and become his submissive 'bad' chick. Then again, why were we told in the Disney movie released in 1989, *The Beauty and the Beast* that Belle who falls for the beast, suddenly cures his aggression in a twist of faith? Then again, you could also see Gaston as the 'alpha' dominant male. Reversibly, the Beast is the hero; nothing is ever what it seems. That is exactly what I'm going to discuss with you here because nothing is ever what it seems. We watch the news and movies; listen to music without realizing that all the while we are being fed subliminal messages like a wire to our brain.

We then interpret the images and words we hear from songs and general media. Then when it is repeated to us it becomes imprinted in our mind and our beliefs. Unfortunately, it has been recognized that the media uses effective means of propaganda to imprint the desired concept in our minds. However, it is not always positive; it is mainly negative. Next time you turn on the radio, listen to each song carefully. Concentrate on the words and don't get distracted by the beat, which we do. Therefore, when you sing the lyrics you never actually interpret their meaning. However, this time really listen to them, or search them online and read them out loud to yourself. How are women presented today in music or movies, in television series even?

Imagine when you first watched Grease for the first time. Did you look up to Sandy in a heroic way? Were you inspired to chase the dominant, 'alpha' male? Is this really what we should be taught as young girls? Therefore, is the media, in effect working to instigate negative behavioral instincts that on a larger scale set out to control us? This is a topic that receives much speculation, especially in recent years; it has sprung up a whole new trend in what you can only describe as controversial conspiracy theories that are believed to be set out to control the human race negatively. However, these are just speculations and can only be viewed in theoretical terms as a possible factor that can contribute to a reason why we might have this belief to always fall for the wrong guy.

5.5. "I've Got to Break Free"

"You can be anything you want to be, just turn yourself into anything you think you could ever be."
(Freddie Mercury)

When women get themselves into a pattern where they fall for the wrong guy all the time; the trick is to break this pattern. However, that is easier said than done because a pattern is not so easy to break when it becomes a habit, or a bad habit should I say. We find ourselves back under its tight snare, which is our biological dependence to follow *'the trend.'* Our beliefs become so intently led in the wrong direction that we become lost in amidst the complicated milestones we find ourselves meeting every time we meet the *wrong* guy. We start to wonder who is the *right* guy is and will he ever be attracted to you...

The answer is yes he will, but only when you are ready to believe that you deserve the *right* guy. The feeling of worthlessness that arises from choosing the *bad* guy is not worth the adrenalin rush, which brings you crashing back down after it's reached its peak. He might decide to ring you up and make you feel special again, but it is always short-lived; isn't it? You might think you crave the instability because of the emotions, which you feel rushing through you every time you see his number calling. However, this instability is unhealthy. You are addicted to the feeling of passion and the sudden rush of adrenalin that is released when it keeps going wrong. The only trouble is you always start off feeling happy and positive, but then end up losing and feeling terrible in the end.

Gradually this addiction for passion, which feeds your desire to go for the *wrong* type will leave you with a completely bleak outlook on love, life and men on the whole. You have set these cogs into motion. Your beliefs are what you have chosen to believe and still do. Therefore, if you want to make a change, which by now you should do. You have to start gaining back your confidence, but also change your beliefs to believe that you are worth something better. The addictive feeling aroused from sex is not love and it is also not healthy for you. Love and happiness lie in a more long-lived, stable, and sustainable relationship.

Chapter 6

UNDERSTANDING THE LOGISTICS OF LOVE

Can you define love?...

O r, is it too complex to even start thinking about, let alone explain? Imagine that you could explain love; would you choose to believe it or keep with your false interpretations of love? The truth is, there are definite logistics to love as a theory or a concept. Although, a little complex at times. However, when you see them in black and white, you can begin to learn and understand them. You start to see the love and your relationships in love with people in a whole new light. Just the realization of what can be defined as love will help you to act differently in love with your partner, or future partners.

However, sometimes we need to take a step back from love, especially if we are suffering the regular trials and tribulations that come with every strong and long-lasting relationship. You need to stop and see it for what it really is. Therefore, in Chapter 6, I will focus on sharing some of the logistics with you. When you look at the greater picture of how *love* works as a driving force to combine the alternate female and male characteristics. Then you start to see, although we share polar characteristics, which clash sometimes in moments of high pressure and stress, then it is intended for a reason. Therefore rather than repel each other. Why not learn to accept each other's differences, recognize them, talk about them, and share your knowledge and understanding of them. This vital realization of fact combined with communication and compromise will often save a marriage from falling apart; when it is not ready to.

Look at it from the Ancient Greek's point of view who saw *love* as having eight segments or definitions, which make up different stages in love. For example, there is the sexual passion that we feel and the Ancient Greeks labeled 'Eros,' which gave birth to the concept of 'eroticism.' Well it is very different from the love that we share with a partner when we reach the long-term partner stage, which is 'Pragma.' Therefore, when we shed light on these theories outlined thousands of years ago in Ancient Greece about *love.* Then we start to realize why some of us become confused that 'Eros,' who is that powerful passionate and sexual drive, is *love.* In other words, sustainable and definite. Well I hate to break it to you 'Eros' is not this. However, maybe a lack of 'Eros' can negatively affect our mental and physical wellbeing, as theorized by T.S. Elliot, in *Lady Chatterley's Lover.* Therefore, an ideal balance would be a mixture of 'Philia's' friendship with the passion of 'Eros,' which makes - 'Pragma.' When you find this in another man you might just have found your soulmate.

What is a soulmate? And do they *really* exist?...

How do you know when you have found yours? When the stars are aligned and the time is right. Well, then you could take a stroll down the street one day and look into someone's eyes and -'Chabang!' You are instantly filled with a glow of passion, as well as familiarity for this person and the feeling seems mutual. When you strike up a conversation; it instantly flows. Then you might have found your soulmate; it's not something you can control, the Earth controls it for you. Then again, you might find your soulmate resting in your compatible star sign. Who knows?...

All I know is, love is very complicated until you chose to understand it and appreciate it for what it is- unrequited support, rather than unlimited suffering!

6.1. Finding a Soul Mate

"He's more myself than I am. Whatever our souls are made of, his and mine are the same."
(Wuthering Heights, Emile Bronte)

So, what is a soulmate then?...

In the romantic novel written by Emily Bronte called *Wuthering Heights,* the female protagonist Cathy proclaims to Nelly that Heathcliff is her soulmate by saying that: "he's more myself than I am. Whatever our souls are made of, his and mine are the same." She wrote this nearly two centuries ago, in 1847. Bronte wrote her outstanding Gothic-Romantic novel claiming that somewhere amongst the spiritual waves and magnetizing energetic vibrations, which make up our world and social network there is someone on our same wavelength that we are meant to be with. They are destined for us. However indefinitely you believe this to be true. Therefore, when you meet someone who you feel like you might have met before, but then you instantly hit it off and it was like the spark was already there; it didn't need any ignition. It could be that you met your soulmate.

I know it's not everyone's cup of tea and neither is astrology, yet astrology signs are an important way of reading love. You are born in a specific month and the basis of your characteristics are aligned to this time. For this reason, you often have a match; but rarely with the same star sign. However, another sign is most certainly destined to be matched to yours; like ylang-ylang. in other words, alike is a perfect match, but then so do opposites attract. It is about finding a perfect balance between these two realms, which is usually your star sign match. Well, if this is the case, then maybe there is a possibility that our future and destiny is mapped out for us. Then possibly our other soul's half is written and aligned somewhere in the stars to appear together and somehow coincide somewhere on Earth.

Soulmates don't necessarily need to be lovers, they can also be best friends, family members even because you share the same blood. Then it is understandable that you will share part of the same soul. When you meet a lover who is your soulmate and who you have the possibility of sharing the rest of your life with. You also get the opportunity to make your perfect 'idealized' family with your connected soul, which will breed more and so the story goes. You will realize you have met your destined soulmate because instant magnetic energy will be produced when you come into contact with each other, which sends instant waves of familiarity to your brain. It might occur the first time you meet, therefore you should know they are meant to know you.

You are lucky if you find your soulmate, but don't spend your life searching for them; the fact is, they will come to you. The Earth will drive you into each other's path when the time is right and it will feel right! It is theorized that your soulmate should share a similar age to you, sometimes maybe just a year or two apart. It is also theorized that certain astrological signs are attracted to each other on a level that can be described as your perfect 'soulmate' material. So what astrological sign are you? Would you like to know who you're love match is?

Okay, so these are the signs that are most likely to be your soulmate in love:

Aries (March 21 - April 19) - Leo, Sagittarius and Libra

Taurus (April 20 - May 20) - Capricorn, Pisces and Scorpio

Gemini (May 21 - June 20) - Libra, Aquarius and Aries

Cancer (June 21 - July 22) - Scorpio, Taurus and Capricorn

Leo (July 23 - August 22) - Aries, Sagittarius and Libra

Virgo (August 23 - September 22) - Taurus, Pisces and Capricorn

Libra (September 23 - October 22) - Aquarius, Gemini and Sagittarius

Scorpio (October 23 - November 21) - Cancer, Capricorn and Taurus

Sagittarius (November 22 - December 21) - Leo, Aries and Libra

Capricorn (December 22 - January 19) - Virgo, Taurus and Cancer

Aquarius (January 20 - February 18) - Libra, Gemini and Sagittarius

Pisces (February 19 - March 20) - Cancer, Taurus and Capricorn

Now you can go by these or not, don't rely on them though because you never really know. It could be your soulmate is a completely different sign altogether. So do not dump your guy, just because he doesn't match up to your astrological sign. I'm sure you match up on a whole of other different levels. It is important not to get too wrapped up and obsess over the idea of meeting and falling in love with your soulmate. It could be that your soulmate is staring you straight in the face, you just haven't realized it yet.

6.2. Men are from Mars and Women are from Venus

"We are two opposite poles of a magnet"
(Angry Bird)

In the non-fiction book by John Gray, *Men are from Mars and Women are from Venus.* Gray insights us to some fresh new ideas on gender equality through his trending psychological non-fiction novel, which highlights the biological differences between male and female characters. He zones in on the behavioral symptoms, which ultimately cause the cataclysm to relationships falling apart, especially during times of difficulty, stress and tension. John Gray's revolutionary theories on love and psychology resound with the title, which has become something of a modern-day colloquial term to label the inexplicable and complicated misunderstandings that arise in a relationship between a man and woman in love, especially when *'times get tough.'* Frequently, what happens is that arguments spiral out of control with one person and irrevocably lay blame on the other. No one reaches a mutual understanding or accepts the other's instinctive flaws.

In his novel, John Gray reports these character clashes as flaws, which rest in our biological DNA, as well as opposing gender roles due to survival. In other words, a woman's 'primal' role is to nurture, but equally feel nurtured during times of hardship and pain. On the contrary, a man will instinctively walk away from a woman who starts to show signs of distress because this is his instinctive norm. So, where the woman expects the opposite, then the man does. We are intended to magnetize, but equally and we are left with our ultimate biological 'catch 22'. This difference irrevocably results in most couples drifting apart, which is when the romance dies out and couples separate. This happens more and more in our liberal modern society. It is a consequence of our misunderstanding and lack of communication in love, as well as a lack of intuition and acceptance of polar gender characteristics, which Gray famously compares to two different planets altogether. There is the cold and impartial God of war, which is Mars embodied by man. Then there is Venus the Goddess of love who embodies the female spirit.

Interestingly, John Gray endured years of research in creating this life-changing book in light of a personal moment, which he shared in an argument with his wife. It sparked an epiphany, which developed from his reaction to the profound differences he observed in his relationship with his wife when they were both under a lot of pressure and stress. He also noticed differences in each of their expectations during moments of tension, which then initiated a sore reaction or perception upon the other when they felt they were unfulfilled. He proposes that this then inspires an inability to understand and connect to each other's reverse reaction because we not in tune with it. Gray's realization enables him to anticipate his wife's reaction much easier. They were able to confront and communicate their differences with each other and move on positively in their relationship. An understanding of each other's basic differential behaviors and perspectives allowed them to regain their love and trust for one another, as well as save their marriage.

Therefore, when you start to see things get tough or you're both under a lot of emotional stress and pressure from work; home-life even. do not be quick to diminish them or start believing that they don't care anymore. Remember John Gray's theory on gender behavioral differences: *Men are from Mars and Women are from Venus,* then try and see your partner in a new light. He is simply following his biological behavioral instinct, which receives a different message to yours. However, complicated and unintelligible it might be to believe that our differences are at times so completely, and uncontrollably polar. They are also very natural. These natural differences make up the whole complex and perfect network of energy that keeps love going, as well as drives and makes life. You always need a happy medium of *positive-negative* energy to keep the world revolving, or to keep a battery-powered; then maybe, you need it to keep a relationship surviving too, you just need to realize and learn to read when things are going wrong and discuss these problems together, but also the reactions that you have to these problems. Tell him you don't *want* a hug but you *need* one!

6.3. The Greek's Theory on Love

"Eros, again now, the loosener of limbs troubles me,
Bittersweet, sly, uncontrollable creature…"
(Sappho)

The art of romance and love has baffled us for centuries, in fact, since the dawn of time. It works in ways that we find it hard to read or understand sometimes, let alone accept. Many of us resign ourselves to thinking that there is no definite truth or logical definition to love; it works with a complete mind of its own. It engulfs us in its merciless snare: binding us, shaking us; then it spits us back out naked and restless on the floor. At times, it does feel like this doesn't it?...

However, it can also be extremely therapeutic and supportive to our human souls. It can breed in us a happiness that is next to nothing; the best feeling in the world. What it does seem like though, is there are different scales and levels of love. The love you feel for your child, mother, or siblings or even friends is very different from the love you share with a lover. There are also a different set of emotions released when you are making love, to when you are giggling and play-fighting on the couch or watching television. Do you think there are different ways to describe love?

Well the Ancient Greeks did. The Ancient Greeks in their epic and revolutionary philosophical era theorized that love has eight separate segments or meanings that define *love* as a whole entity of love. They proclaim them to work alongside, but also against each other, sometimes combining but always separate:

1. Agape - all enduring, self-less love and unconditional love felt by god

2. Philia - love found in friendship

3. Storge - Love shared in family

4. Pragma - Love shared with a life long partner

5. Philautia - Self-love

6. Ludus - Playful love

7. Mania - Obsession

8. Eros - Sexual passion

The four definitions we will be looking at more closely is:

1. Agape

2. Storge

3. Philia

4. Eros

Let's present them in a diagram to give an even better understanding of how the four concepts of love work to connect and define each other in one big complex framework that we can call love.

(DIAGRAM OF LOVE)

Where Agape, Storge and Philia inspire sustainability, durability and promote security; they are part of the subconscious catalyst to love. Then eros, or 'erotic' love, can be associated as the 'romantic' and physical reaction to love, which releases adrenaline aroused through the feelings of ecstasy. This is fuelled by highly emotive stimuli from intimate physical contact and emotional release, which often confuses our mind with a sustainable love. However, it is our natural instinctive emotions that act on a momentous passion that misleads us thinking that this excitement, or ecstasy released from 'erotic' love is a definite love, which it is not. Have you ever found yourself with a new partner that you have been sharing intimate time with; you might have an extra hot, passionate night together but it's still early days. You barely even know him yet; you've spent more time in between the sheets getting to know his physical side to finding out what his hobbies are, what his favorite movie or even his favorite food is! You know nothing about this secret lover of yours, except you find yourself screaming 'I love you' at him during sex when emotions reach their phenomenal peak!

When this sounds familiar, then you know you have been fooled by that all-defying, impermanent feeling that is aroused by Eros. Normally, these romances are very short-lived and one month down the line you've fallen out and you're not talking anymore; and both seeing new people. Therefore, when you cried your love out for him; it couldn't have been that set in stone. As the famous female, lesbian Ancient Greek poet, Sappho, once wrote in one of her legendary lyric poems: *"Eros, again now, the loosener of limbs troubles me, Bittersweet, sly, uncontrollable creature..."* She in fact, diminishes this feeling of short-lived eroticism for raising a sort of false recognition of love through romance and physical intimacy. She calls it a '[troublesome]... Bittersweet, sly, uncontrollable creature.' One that should not be depended upon, and which can be destructive and de-harmonize the sustainability that arouses out of the other three definitions of love.

In other words, a partner who is either male and female may start to crave Eros to feed their desire for natural adrenaline and eroticism. They may also get confused in thinking that this is true love. This is where the high number of infidelity occurs between couples, once they reach the stage of Pragma. They begin to associate Pragma's unconditional love that is shared between two life long partners as being something that is too comfortable and boring because it misses sexual passion. Therefore, they instinctively go looking for the feeling of 'Eros.' It also presents a reason as to why women may get stuck in the 'honeymoon' zone and always find herself in dead-end relationships. She misinterprets the intense emotions that arise in passionate sex and the excitement that is aroused in the preliminary stages of love as something, as a sort of everlasting love; when it is not! They may decide to read the emotive stimuli and start showing stronger feelings of love towards that person, which instead scares them away. This is because men react quite differently to these emotions. After all, they have a much higher, required sexual drive. It is not just a feeling to them, it is a necessity. Therefore, they will constantly search for the 'Eros' to satisfy their highly strung sexual release.

However, when we go back to T.S. Elliot's ground-breaking novel Lady Chatterley's Lover and see that Constance is missing this passionate Eros, as a way of completing her mind, body and soul. Then looking at the diagram where Philia and Eros cross to become Pragma. You can start to understand that a balance of these two definitions of love will determine the sustainability and durability of love with your partner. Then the psychology of love might be complex, but when you see it in a black and white pictogram it becomes a little easier to understand. When you separate it into these four, or even segments that make up the much greater picture, which is love.

Made in the USA
Middletown, DE
18 June 2020